SPY TOYS

A Pictorial History and Price Guide

Written by Cramer Burks

The Windmill Group

THE WINDMILL GROUP, INC.
P.O. Box 56551
Sherman Oaks, California 91413

First Edition

Manufactured in the United States of America

Published by The Windmill Group, Inc., P.O. Box 56551, Sherman Oaks, California 91413
Telephone (818) 704-6650   FAX (818) 704-6655   E-Mail: info@windmillgroup.com

ISBN: 1-887790-04-7

Publisher's Cataloging in Publication
(Prepared by Quality Books Inc.)

Burks, Cramer.
    Spy toys : a pictorial history and price guide / written by Cramer
Burks. -- 1st ed.
    p. cm.
    Preassigned LCCN: 98-
    ISBN: 1-887790-04-7

    1. Toys--United States--History. 2. Sears, Roebuck and
Company--Catalogs. I. Sears, Roebuck and Company. II.
Title

TS2301.T7B87 1999   688.7'2
                                                          QBI98-798

*Front cover photograph: A young super-sleuth strikes a spy-like pose with his James Bond 007 Pistol while playing with his
Gilbert/Sears James Bond Road Race Set and Man From U.N.C.L.E. Board Game. (Model: Brett Fisher)
Rear cover photographs: A youngster readies his spy toys to fight off pretend bad guys. (Model: Chad Seaman)
A display of spy-related toy merchandise targeted to kids of the Sixties. (Photograph courtesy Bill Bruegman/Toy Scouts, Inc.)*

NOTICE

**ALL TITLES, CHARACTERS, LOGOS, PRODUCT NAMES,
BRAND NAMES AND THE LIKE DEPICTED IN THIS BOOK
AND RELATED MATERIALS ARE EITHER TRADE NAMES,
TRADEMARKS OR REGISTERED TRADEMARKS
OF AND OWNED BY THE RESPECTIVE OWNERS.**

For Heather, Chad and Morgan

The three most important kids in my life.

Growing up doesn't mean you have to lose the child in you.

Acknowledgments

The following people were kind enough to donate their services, offer invaluable advice or allow me access to their collections during the making of this book:

Mike DeWinter

Brett Chapman

Marianne Nave

Jerry O'Brien

Chad Seaman

Myles Stievater

Doug Redenius

...and my good friend Tom Holland, without whom this volume would not be possible.

Foreword

The idea of spying on one other has been around for thousands of years. The Aztecs did it, the Romans did it and even before them the Chinese mastered it into an art form. Espionage was always a quiet practice though. We knew it was there and usually necessary, but we left it to faceless men hiding in shadows in faraway countries.

But when James Bond hit movie theaters in 1962, spies and spying came right to our neighborhoods! And so did the toys... fantastic plastic devices which allowed every 12-year old to fulfill their own fantasies of international intrigue. Now, any boy or girl with a 007 briefcase or pistol or code book could save the world from certain destruction. Soon, the proliferation of movie and TV spies brought hundreds of spy-oriented toys into stores and mail-order catalogs, a deluge that continues to this day. So why have spy toys become so popular and so collectible? Because they're cool... that's why!

Take, for instance, a small car with an ejector seat and machine guns that pop out from the front. Or a toy briefcase that contains hidden compartments and secret knives and cameras. Or after-shave lotion just like my favorite spy wears. I don't know about you, but for me that's neat. If my use of the words "cool" and "neat" sound a little dated it's because all these terrific collectibles date from the mid-Sixties... and those terms seem to fit even today.

When you flip through this wonderful book, you will take a trip back in time. Who could have predicted the merchandising that would follow when James Bond, The Man From U.N.C.L.E., Our Man Flint and other spy heroes were born. No one could have envisioned the toys, games, puzzles, clothing, jewelry, magazines, books, dolls, cars, records, tapes, posters and so on and so on.

If you owned all of what is found within the pages of this book you would be a very rich person today. Some of these collectibles can run into thousands of dollars. Try going to a toy show or bidding electronically for some of these toys and you'll find they cost as much as the government spends on real spy gadgets! Old toys can be a good investment though, if you know what to look for.

SPY TOYS will prove valuable to you in several ways. It's great to see never-before-published pictures of some really rare toys. And, the book also makes a good reference to collectibles you might otherwise have passed by. But most of all use the book for your own pleasure... perhaps to remind you of those childhood days when *you too* saved the world from certain destruction.

DOUG REDENIUS
Collector and Vice-President of the Ian Fleming Foundation

Introduction

May, 1963 - James Bond, Agent 007 of Her Majesty's Secret Service made his debut in the United States with the release of the motion picture "DR. NO." Within a year and a half, Bond would become one of the most heavily promoted and produced toy collectible characters in history, with a plethora of television and movie spies close behind.

Years before the term "mass merchandising" became synonymous with so-called "blockbuster" films like "Star Wars," "Batman," "Indiana Jones" and others, James Bond blazed a merchandising trail that has become a tremendous array of highly desirable collectibles today.

By early 1965, the spy toy boom was in full force, with fellow agents Maxwell Smart, Napoleon Solo, Illya Kuryakin, John Drake, James West and others populating toy stores all over the world.

As for me, Christmas 1965 brought the first of many 007 toys I would eventually own. To this day I can remember ripping away the gift wrap and packaging to discover the coolest toy I had ever owned... the MPC James Bond Briefcase! Inside were a hidden knife, a break-apart sniper's rifle, even an exploding cap device ready to blow up some unknown enemy if my secret case was opened. It was just like the movies I loved so much. Little did I realize this present from my parents would turn into a hobby that, more than thirty years later, would show no signs of subsiding.

Growing up in the Sixties, many were the allowance dollars that were spent on "Man From U.N.C.L.E." gum cards, "Wild, Wild West" comic books, "Avengers" paperbacks, not to mention plastic models, puzzles, action figures and more.

As my teen years passed, some of my collection survived the rigors of childhood spy encounters. Some were played with until there was nothing left but trash while the rest were lost to periodic search-and-destroy room cleanings by my mother. Besides, I soon found that as my income grew my spending habits changed. Real cars became more important than car models and the latest clothes much more desirable than comic books and games.

When I reached my mid-Thirties, I realized, as many of my fellow Baby Boomers have, just what great toys (and now hot collectibles) we had grown up with. Even if you didn't experience these wonderful toys as a child, I hope this book will give you a hint how much fun the toys of the Cold War could be.

Be you a die-hard collector or a beginner... or somewhere in between... perhaps this book will help in hunting down the spy toys you want. Of course, always remember that toys can be a terrific investment but they're still toys... and that means having fun.

Cramer Burks

About this price guide

PRICING

The values of the items listed in this book were derived from a number of sources including market-checking, cross-referencing and shopping various toy and collectible dealers. My own experience as a long time collector of toys and memnorabilia also helped me arrive at realistic prices. Surely one can find any of the collectibles in this book at higher or lower prices, depending on a wide range of market conditions.

Toy auctions were not factored into my values, as I beleive these types of transactiuons are frequently over-inflated.

Finally, when buying a specific collectible, an individual may be willing to pay more than market price, be it for sentiment, nostalgia or investment.

CONDITION

Most of the spy toy collectibles in this guide are graded as Good to Mint condition. "Mint" is a very misused term in the toy world. For our grading purposes a Mint item is nothing less than perfect - still sealed, no flaws, no blemishes and fuully complete. Anything less is NOT "Mint."

"Very Good" to "Near Mint" is an item that is complete but may, for instance, have no sealas in many car model kits,. A small flaw or mark on the packaging is usually acceptable.

For collectibles in lesser condition, one must use their own judgement and discretion as to the items value.

EXCLUSIONS

Very few foreign-made items have been included in this guide. I chose to focus on toys made available through U.S. distribution and realistically available to collectors.

Excluded from this volume are certain borderline spy shows, films and cartoons like T.H.E. CAT, IT TAKES A THIEF, AMOS BURKE, SECRET AGENT and JAMES BOND JR.

NOTE

These values and price ranges are to be used only as rough guides and the author and the publisher do not guarantee any particular value or price range as to any item.

The Incredible, Collectible World of 007

"Bond, James Bond." Classic lines of dialogue that still thrill moviegoers almost 40 years after they were first spoken by Sean Connery, the original 007.

The James Bond film series produced a treasure trove of wonderful toys. Today, they are collectible classics and are some of the most popular... and costly... collector toys on the market.

Although some Bond film tie-ins were made early on, 1964 through 1966 was the heyday of Bond-mania when it came to items. But 007 toys continue to be made today and each new movie released generates a wave of new collectibles.

Apparently, not only diamonds are forever... but so are James Bond collectibles.

1. **DR. NO   COMIC BOOK**
   D.C. Comics (1963) *Left, top*

The first James Bond collectible, this one-shot comic was based on the movie with just a few plot changes included. As an example the "Three Blind Mice" are white men, not black men.

VG to Mint $75-$125

2. **JAMES BOND SECRET AGENT 007 BOARD GAME**
   Milton-Bradley (1965) *Left, center*

A very common collectible, this game was produced in two versions. The first has a generic-looking Bond on the box cover. The second has a likeness of Sean Connery. Values for both games are the same.

VG to Mint $20-$50

3. **GOLDFINGER JAMES BOND BOARD GAME**
   Milton-Bradley (1965) *Left, bottom*

The second 007 board game produced. Players attempt to move their spies into Fort Knox before their opponents. Great graphics on the box lid make this item popular with collectors.

VG to Mint $60-$100

4. THUNDERBALL
   JAMES BOND BOARD GAME
   Milton-Bradley (1965) *Right*

Another beautifully illustrated game, inside and out. Players try to uncover several hi-jacked atom bombs fighting S.P.E.C.T.R.E. along the way. Deciphering the secret signals is the key to winning this game.

VG to Mint $40-$60

5. MESSAGE FROM M
   JAMES BOND BOARD GAME
   Ideal Toys (1965) *Right*

The rarest and most valuable Bond board game, this oversized piece has Dr. No, Goldfinger and Largo as foes of the game player.

VG to Mint $150-$200

6. JAMES BOND 007 CARD GAME
   Milton-Bradley (1965) *Right*

A nice color photo from GOLDFINGER graces the cover of this small game.

VG to Mint $40-$50

7. ENTER THE DANGEROUS WORLD OF JAMES BOND CARD GAME
   Milton-Bradley (1965) *Right*

This item comes in a nice black box, with a gold lithograph of Sean Connery on the front. A dice game!

VG to Mint $40-$50

8. GOLDFINGER PUZZLE
Milton-Bradley (1965) *Left, top*

"Bond's Bullets Blaze." This 600+ piece puzzle is a painting of Bond's fight with Goldfinger's henchmen at his Swiss factory.

Sealed $60
Mint but opened $40

9. GOLDFINGER PUZZLE
Milton-Bradley (1965) *Left, center*

"Fort Knox Finale." Another 600+ piece puzzle, this one depicts Bond and Oddjob's duel to the death.

Sealed $60
Mint but opened $40

Front

Back

10. GOLDFINGER PUZZLE
Milton-Bradley (1965) *Above, left and right*

"Golden Girl." This item came in a large black box with the puzzle picture printed on the back. Bond and the gold-painted Jill Masterson are painted on a gold backing.

11. THUNDERBALL PUZZLE
Milton-Bradley (1965) *Right, top*

"Bond's Battle." The most visually stunning of the Milton-Bradley Puzzles, this one features Connery fighting a S.P.E.C.T.R.E. frogman with the underwater battle going on in the background.

Good to MIB $40-60

12. THUNDERBALL PUZZLE
Milton-Bradley (1965) *Right, center*

"S.P.E.C.T.R.E.'s Surprise." Another underwater scene of the Aquatroopers and S.P.E.C.T.R.E. frogmen, but minus 007.

Good to MIB $40-60

Front

Back

13. THUNDERBALL PUZZLE
Milton-Bradley (1965) *Above, left and right*

This red-boxed puzzle is the rarest of the puzzle sets. Double-sided, it featured Bond's classic speargun pose with three bathing beauties and the reverse featured a painting of Domino.

VG to MIB $75-$100

Two Tie-Ins From
PHILADELPHIA CHEWING GUM CORP.

1. JAMES BOND SECRET AGENT 007 BUBBLE GUM sells for a nickel everywhere, under the "SWELL" brand label. It is packaged in special JAMES BOND boxes with a FREE official 007 badge offer on every colorful wrapper.
2. TRADING CARDS, also packaged under the "SWELL" brand name, are sold without the gum and the kids flip over them, *pun intended!*

Dealers have all kinds of display material, including the streamer pictured here. Gum and trading cards have been big movie merchandisers since the industry began. This is one of your greatest away-from-theatre tie-in opportunities. Tie it up locally now.

For further information, contact:

GABRIEL'S Walkie-Talkie Set

This incredible top actually works effectively up to 300 feet! There are two units, each a sending-receiving set, with three transistor press-talk circuits. Complete with batteries, antennas and 90 day warranty, the set comes in a full color display box with James Bond 007 motif.

Gabriel has set a media buy which includes magazines, newspapers and spot TV. For local advertising, it has supplied all its dealers with one and two column ad mats, catalogues and other display material.

For further information, contact:

This two-way treasure is worth about $125-$150 if *Mint in Box.*

MILTON BRADLEY Games and Puzzles!

One of the foremost manufacturers of games for both children and adults, Milton Bradley, has developed four games and six jigsaw puzzles for James Bond tie-ins. Copy on the well-packaged box of one invites the buyer to "Enter the dangerous world of James Bond . . . play if you dare!" The others are superbly tailored to the Bond idea of sophisticated gamesmanship . . . with skill, luck and daring all coming into the play. Fun for the children as well as men and women, these games are richly designed for impressive gift-giving. With the puzzles, they comprise a great tie-in combination that should get you entire window and counters.

Milton Bradley Company will advertise in major magazines and newspapers and has allocated a Bond budget for spot television.

For further information, contact:

14. 007 ELECTRIC DRAWING SET
Lakeside (1965) *Left*

A nice portrait of Sean Connery as James Bond adorns this set, which includes a plastic tracing board, pencils, sharpener and "Adventure Sheets."

Good to Mint $125-$150

15. JAMES BOND MODEL KIT
Aurora (1966) *Left and right*

This famous model kit not only boasts a great diorama of 007, but a neat painting of Bond on the box lid too.

Built-up model $125
Mint in Box $250-$300

16. ODD JOB MODEL KIT
Aurora (1966) *Left and right*

Another great Aurora kit, and rarer than the Bond model above.

Built-up model $125-$150
Mint in Box $350-$400

17. ASTON-MARTIN SUPER SPY CAR
Aurora (1966)   *Right, top*

Aurora did not get the license to use James Bond for this model, but it is still a great 007 item.

Built-up Model $25
Mint in Box $100

18. JAMES BOND ASTON-MARTIN DB-5 KIT
Airfix (1965)   *Right, center*

The "Officially Licensed James Bond Car Kit."

Built-up Model $50-$60
Mint in Box $200-$225

19. JAMES BOND VS. ODDJOB KIT
Airfix (1965)   *Not illustrated.*

So-so box artwork, figures that don't resemble the intended characters... and what you have is a valuable collectible.   *Mint $125-$175*

20. LITTLE NELLIE GYROCOPTER KIT
Airfix (1967)   *Not illustrated.*

The rarest Airfix kit, this model from YOU ONLY LIVE TWICE is easily worth $350 to $400 if mint.

21. JAMES BOND TOYOTA 2000 KIT
Airfix (1967)   *Not illustrated.*

Another great-looking kit from YOU ONLY LIVE TWICE, this item is worth $150 built-up; $400-$450 if MIB.

22. JAMES BOND 007 LUNCHBOX
Aladdin (1966)   *Right, bottom*

This steel box depicts the Aston-Martin on one side, the Disco-Volante on the other. The thermos has the THUNDERBALL underwater battle pictured on it.

Good to Mint $100-$125

23. BOND "XX" LUNCHBOX
Ohio Art (1966)   *Not illustrated.*

A classy box by any standard. Produced in 1966 and 1967, but no thermos was issued in either year. The 1966 version is worth $150 if mint; the 1967 version a bit less at $100.

**24. JAMES BOND 007
GUM CARD SET**
Philadelphia (1965) *Left, top*

Nine samples are pictured at left from
a 66-card set of black-and-white stills
from DR. NO, FROM RUSSIA
WITH LOVE and GOLDFINGER.

Complete mint set $125
Wrapper (right) $40-$50
Display Box (lower right) $100-$125
Display Sign (lower left) $100-$125

**25. THUNDERBALL
GUM CARD SET**
Philadelphia (1965) *Left, center*

Nine samples are pictured at left from a 66-card set of black-
and-white stills from THUNDERBALL. A decoder was
enclosed for secret messages found on the card backs.

Complete mint set $175
Wrapper (below) $50-$60
Display Box (not illustrated) $150
Display Sign (not illustrated) $175

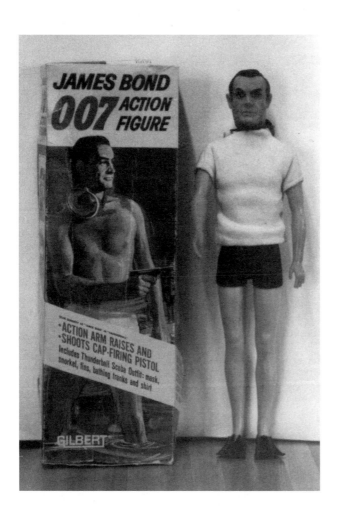

26. JAMES BOND PUPPET FIGURE
    Gilbert (1965)   *Above, right*

A rubber likeness, albeit not the most flattering, of Sean Connery.

Mint in Package $75-$100

27. ODDJOB PUPPET FIGURE
    Gilbert (1965)   *Not illustrated.*

Similar rubber puppet of Harold Sakata as Oddjob. Value is about the same as above puppet.

28. JAMES BOND ACTION FIGURE #2
    Gilbert (1965)   *Above, left*

A 12" likeness of Sean Connery, this is a premiere Bond collectible. A face mask, snorkel, swimfins and a pistol came with the figure. The box has great artwork with black and white photos decorating the sides.

Mint in Box $200-$225

29. ODDJOB ACTION FIGURE
    Gilbert (1965)   *Right, bottom*

The companion to the Bond figure, also graced with neat box decoration. A deadly derby and karate outfit were issued with the figure.

Mint in Box $350-$400

JAMES BOND
SECRET AGENT
007

ACTION FIGURES

16101 JAMES BOND 007 ACTION FIGURE. He's only a foot tall or so, but it's James Bond himself, exactly as he appears in the thrilling new movie "Thunderball" — with scuba mask, snorkel, swim fins, trunks, shirt. He holds Baretta pistol that fires a cap (caps not furnished) when you release his arm. And take a look at all the fantastic outfits you can get for him!

16111 ODDJOB ACTION FIGURE. He's that real creepy character from "Goldfinger"— 11" of deadly menace! Place Oddjob's "steel" derby in his hand, pull arm back and release, hat flies out to cut down his victim — just as in the movie. Left arm has authentic Karate chop action. He comes in white Karate outfit with colorful neck cloth, head band and black belt.

Exciting JAMES BOND Action Apparel and Accessories

16251 DISGUISE KIT. Includes: 2 different masks, hand grenade that fires caps (caps not included), trench coat, black pants, shoes and hat, dark glasses, eye patch and operating binoculars.

16253 DELUXE SCUBA OUTFIT. Includes authentic miniatures of eye-popping apparatus used by Bond in the movies: Scuba vehicle for underwater propulsion; Action Spear Gun that fires 3 different type projectiles; scuba air tanks; orange scuba jacket and headpiece with detachable decoy duck on top.

16255 DISGUISE KIT No. 2. Includes 2 masks plus cap-firing pistol with kit for conversion to rifle, grenade belt with 4 grenades, and ammo pouch.

16252 "THUNDERBALL" SET. Includes: replica of famous Jump Set pack (used by Bond to fly over walls and buildings), Tommy gun that fires caps (caps not included), long-sleeve white shirt, black pants and shoes.

16254 SCUBA OUTFIT No. 2. Includes: Scuba jacket, headpiece with decoy duck on top, spring-action spear gun and 3 spears, and dagger.

16256 SCUBA OUTFIT No. 3. Includes: Air tanks, tubes, bracket and dagger.

16257 SCUBA OUTFIT No. 4. Includes: Spring-action spear gun, 3 spears, underwater propulsion unit.

Send for free catalog showing other exciting GILBERT TOYS!

Gilbert also makes famous Erector, "All Aboard" landscaped train sets, racing sets, microscopes, chemistry sets and telescopes. Write to: The A. C. Gilbert Co., 007 Erector Square, New Haven, Conn.

30. JAMES BOND ACTION APPAREL KIT
   Gilbert (1965)   *Opposite page*

For the 12" doll, this accessory kit includes a spear gun, knife and air tanks. *Not illustrated.*

Mint in Package $60-$80

31. JAMES BOND DISGUISE KIT #1
   Gilbert (1965)   *Opposite page*

This set includes two different masks, trench coat, black pants, shoes and hat, sunglasses, an eye patch and binoculars.

Mint in Package $125

32. JAMES BOND DISGUISE KIT #2
   Gilbert (1965)   *Opposite page*

Two masks, a cap-firing pistol with a rifle-conversion kit, a 4-grenade belt and ammo pouch make up this pack.

Mint in Package $125

33. JAMES BOND DELUXE SCUBA OUTFIT
   Gilbert (1965)   *Opposite page*

This great set has a scuba vehicle, spear gun with three different projectiles, an orange scuba jacket and a head piece with a duck decoy on top.

Mint in Package $125

34. JAMES BOND THUNDERBALL SET
   Gilbert (1965)   *Opposite page*

The most desirable Gilbert accessory set has the famous jet pack, a machine gun, long sleeve white shirt, black pants and shoes.

Mint in Package $150

35. JAMES BOND SCUBA OUTFIT #2
   Gilbert (1965)   *Opposite page*

The duck decoy, headpiece, spring-action speargun with three spears, as well as a dagger are included in this set.

Mint in Package $125

36. JAMES BOND SCUBA OUTFIT #3
   Gilbert (1965)   *Opposite page*

This mini-set comes with air tanks, tubes, bracket and dagger.

Mint in Package $75

37. JAMES BOND SCUBA OUTFIT #4
   Gilbert (1965)   *Opposite page*

The spear gun with three spear attachments and the underwater propulsion kit make up this abbreviated accessory pack.

Mint in Package $75

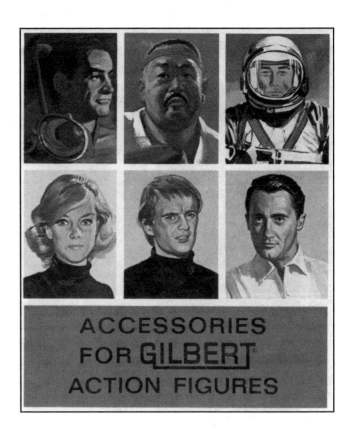

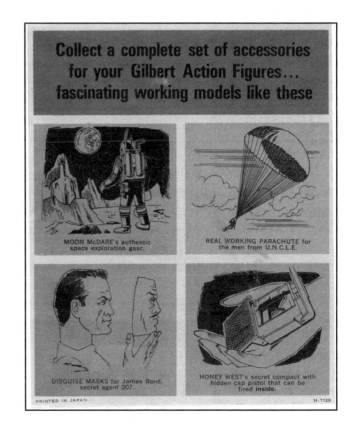

Display Box Header Card for Gilbert Toys

The following Gilbert Figures are each valued at $15, Mint on Card

38. JAMES BOND 3" SCUBA FIGURE
Gilbert (1965)

39. JAMES BOND 3" TUXEDO FIGURE
Gilbert (1965)

40. JAMES BOND 3" FIGURE WITH RIFLE
Gilbert (1965)

41. GOLDFINGER 3" FIGURE
Gilbert (1965)

42. DR. NO 3" FIGURE
Gilbert (1965)

43. LARGO 3" FIGURE
Gilbert (1965)

44. ODDJOB 3" FIGURE
Gilbert (1965)

45. 'M' 3" FIGURE
Gilbert (1965)

46. MISS MONEYPENNY 3" FIGURE
Gilbert (1965)

47. DOMINO 3" FIGURE
Gilbert (1965)

Items 38 and 39

Above: Items 38 and 43   Right: Items 44 and 42

48. JAMES BOND TEN FIGURE SET
Gilbert (1965)

A nice display box is included with all ten figures.

Mint in Package $100-$125

49. JAMES BOND ACTION SET #1
Gilbert (1965) *Not illustrated*

Bond in scuba suit, Largo and the Disco Volante Hydrofoil are included.

Mint in Box $75-$100

50. JAMES BOND ACTION SET #2
Gilbert (1965)

Bond in tuxedo, Miss Moneypenny, 'M' and 'M's desk.

Mint in Box $75-$100

51. JAMES BOND ACTION SET #3
Gilbert (1965)

007 on the Laser Table, Dr. No, Goldfinger and Oddjob figures.

Mint in Box $75-$100

52. JAMES BOND ACTION SET #4
Gilbert (1965) *Not illustrated*

James Bond with rifle, Dr. No and Domino figures.

Mint in Box $75-100

53. JAMES BOND TOY SET #1
Gilbert (1965) *Not illustrated*

This set has a miniature Dragon Tank from DR. NO plus the Disco Volante from THUNDERBALL.

Mint on Card $50

54. JAMES BOND TOY SET #2
Gilbert (1965)

The rotating Secret Map Pool Table, as well as the GOLDFINGER Laser Beam Table are in this nicely boxed set.

Mint on Card $50

55. JAMES BOND TOY SET #3
Gilbert (1965)

'M's desk for the 3" figure, plus an attache case with cap-firing pistol for the 12" Bond Action Figure comprise this set.

Mint on Card $50

Item 54

Item 51

Item 50

Item 55

56. JAMES BOND'S ASTON-MARTIN BATTERY OPERATED
Gilbert (1965) *Right, top and center*

This fully functional 12" replica of the most famous car in the world is a highly desirable colectible. The car features a working ejector seat, bullet-proof shield that raises and lowers, hidden front bumper machine guns that flash and produce sound, extending crash bumpers, revolving license plates, extending tire cutters and bump-and-go forward drive.

When found in Original Box $350-$400

57. THUNDERBALL PILLOWCASE
PFZ (1965) *Not illustrated*

A very rare item, this pillowcase has various Bond action scenes depicted on it and comes in an attractive plastic wrap with "007" printed on it.

Mint in Package $175-$200

58. THUNDERBALL BEACH TOWEL
PFZ (1965) *Not illustrated*

"007" in huge red letters are printed on this large white towel along with a picture of Sean Connery, pistol in hand.

Mint in Package $50-$75

59. THE JAMES BOND BOX
Manufacturer unknown (1965) *Not illustrated*

A very rare dice game. Seldom seen.

VG to Mint $80-$100

60. JAMES BOND HUSHPUPPY SHOES
Hushpuppy (1965) *Not illustrated*

Definately a mint-in-box item, these puppies are costly.

Mint in Box $175-$200

**61.   JAMES BOND SPY WATCH
        WITH DECODER**
        Gilbert (1965) *Right*

A very rare 007 collectible, this watch came "with secret sighting lenses and world time guide."

VG to Mint $325-$350

62.   JAMES BOND LOOSE-LEAF BINDER
        Manufacturer unknown (1965) *Not illustrated*

This solid black three-ring binder has a nice graphic of Sean Connery on the cover.

Good to Mint $50-$75

63.   JAMES BOND SPY TRICKS
        Gilbert (1965) *Not illustrated*

A very attractive box featuring Sean Connery contains ten different magic tricks, all of which involve cards and various keys, gun and other items included with the set.

Good to Mint in Box $100-$125

64.   JAMES BOND VAPOR PAPER AND ACTION PEN
        American Character (1965) *See TV Commercial*

Nice graphics on a blister pack containg vanishing paper, a versatile pen that shoots projectiles, has a secret whistle, writes secret messages and even has a a cap-firing booby trap device.

VG to Mint $75-$100

65.   JAMES BOND RADIO SPOTS
        Various Manufacturers (1964-1966) *Not illustrated*

These rare 33 1/3 r.p.m. records were distributed to radio strations for advertising purposes for all the early Bond films. Ten, twenty, thirty and sixty second spots were included.

Good to Mint $75-$100, but early discs may run higher

66. JAMES BOND 007 ROADRACE SET
   Gilbert (1965) *Above; also see illustrations on cover and in Sears Catalog Pages*

The quintessential Bond collectible. Sold exclusively by Sears, Roebuck and Co. in their stores and in the 1965 Sears Christmas Wishbook, this magnificent set was made up of six interlocking panels which held all the scenery: mountains, lakes, treacherous curves... even an oil slick! Bond's Aston-Martin raced against a red Mustang fastback, at one point in the course leaping a washed out bridge. Unfortunately the set was rushed into production in the Orient and had loads of technical faults. Virtually all the sets were returned to Gilbert, who destroyed them. This major recall bankrupted the venerable 100+ year old Gilbert Toy Company. Complete roadrace sets are extremely scarce today.

VG to Mint $600-$1,000, more if with original box

**67. JAMES BOND ASTON-MARTIN
   SLOT CAR**
   Gilbert (1965) *Right*

For the Gilbert James Bond Road Race Set.

VG to Mint $75-$100

**68. JAMES BOND ASTON-MARTIN
   SLOT CAR**
   Strombecker (1968) *Not illustrated*

Another version of Bond's DB5, ready to take to your neighborhood slot track.

VG to Mint $175-$225

69.   007 GLASS JEWELRY
       Marvin (1965) *Not illustrated*

These rare items came in a black "007" logo box.
Cufflink and Tie Bar Set   *Good to Mint $150-$170*
Cufflink and Tie Tack Set   *Good to Mint $150-$170*
Money Clip   *Good to Mint $100-$125*
Tie Tack   *Good to Mint $80-$100*
Tie Bar   *Good to Mint $80-$100*

70.   JAMES BOND UNDERWATER KIT
       Voit (1965) *Right*

A spy-ready diving mask and snorkel blaster (it shoots water)
were packaged in an attractive box. Swim fins, masks and
snorkels were also available separately. Voit supplied the real
underwater gear for the making of THUNDERBALL.

Good to Mint in Box $50-$75

71.   JAMES BOND CODE-A-MATIC
       Multiple (1965) *See Catalog Pages*

A small plastic 007 code book.

Mint in Package $60

72.   JAMES BOND SECRET 7 RIFLE/PISTOL
       Multiple (1965) *See Catalog Pages*

"The Complete Arsenal" comes in a smart package including
cards, silencer, and super-scope.

Mint in Box $225-$250

73.   JAMES BOND S/A AUTOMATIC PISTOL
       Multiple (1965) *See Catalog Pages*

This item has the standard 007 logo packaging.

VG to Mint $200-$250

74.   JAMES BOND 007 BOND-O-MATIC WATER PISTOL
       Multiple (1965) *Right*

Not just your every day water pistol, this one was authorized by 007!

Mint in Package $75

75.   JAMES BOND PERSONAL ATTACK KIT
       Multiple (1965) *See Catalog Pages*

This gun set, also known as the "P.A.K. Set," comes in an attractive display
box.

Mint in Box $125-$150

76.   JAMES BOND 007 RADIO TRAP
       Multiple (1965) *See Catalog Pages*

"Secret Business Cards" come with this neat item.

Mint in Box $125

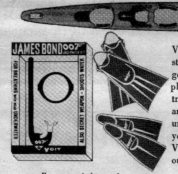

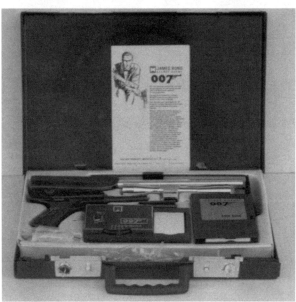

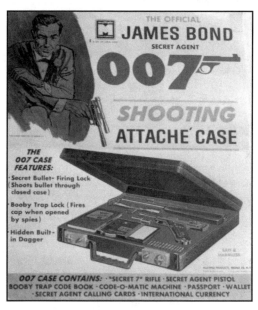

77. JAMES BOND 007 ATTACHE CASE
Multiple (1965) *See also Catalog Pages*

This highly desirable toy contains a disassembled sniper's rifle, code book, passport, hidden throwing knife and a booby-trap mechanism. Finding a mint example of one of these great sets, with all the pieces intact, is becoming quite difficult.

VG to Mint $450-$500
Original Store Display Poster $250

78. BOND ASSAULT RAIDER KIT (B.A.R.K.)
Multiple (1965) *See also Catalog Pages*

This second attache case comes with a rocket launcher, three rockets and a pistol which fires either a "message missile" or exploding grenade. A small cap-firing gun is also included. Originally priced at $5.99, its value has skyrocketed.

JAMES BOND 007 ACCESSORIES

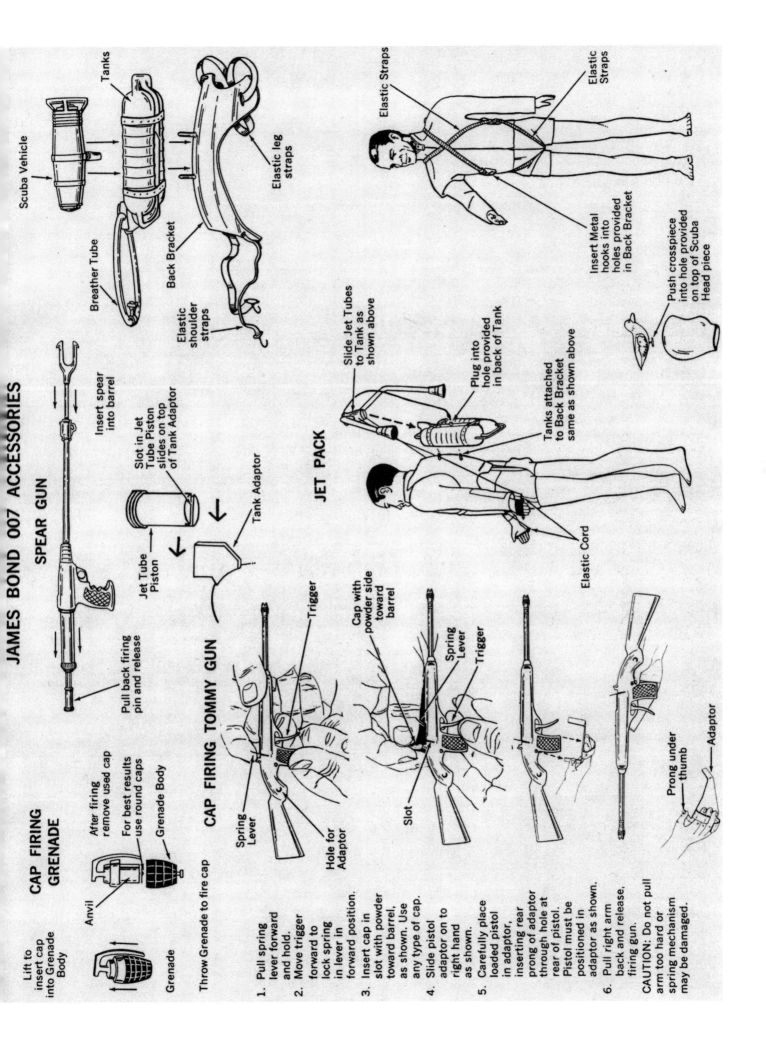

Scuba Vehicle

Tanks

Breather Tube

Back Bracket

Elastic shoulder straps

Elastic leg straps

Elastic Straps

Elastic Straps

Insert Metal hooks into holes provided in Back Bracket

Push crosspiece into hole provided on top of Scuba Head piece

SPEAR GUN

Insert spear into barrel

Slot in Jet Tube Piston slides on top of Tank Adaptor

Tank Adaptor

Jet Tube Piston

Pull back firing pin and release

JET PACK

Slide Jet Tubes to Tank as shown above

Plug into hole provided in back of Tank

Tanks attached to Back Bracket same as shown above

Elastic Cord

CAP FIRING GRENADE

Lift to insert cap into Grenade Body

After firing remove used cap

For best results use round caps

Grenade Body

Grenade

Anvil

Throw Grenade to fire cap

CAP FIRING TOMMY GUN

Trigger

Spring Lever

Hole for Adaptor

Cap with powder side toward barrel

Spring Lever

Trigger

Slot

Prong under thumb

Adaptor

1. Pull spring lever forward and hold.
2. Move trigger forward to lock spring in lever in forward position.
3. Insert cap in slot with powder toward barrel, as shown. Use any type of cap.
4. Slide pistol adaptor on to right hand as shown.
5. Carefully place loaded pistol in adaptor, inserting rear prong of adaptor through hole at rear of pistol. Pistol must be positioned in adaptor as shown.
6. Pull right arm back and release, firing gun.

CAUTION: Do not pull arm too hard or spring mechanism may be damaged.

79. JAMES BOND 007 BOOBY-TRAP EXPLODING CODE BOOK
    Multiple (1965) *See Catalog Pages*

This single item toy from Multiple has really blown up in cost today.

Good to Mint $100-$125

80. JAMES BOND-X AUTOMATIC SHOOTING CAMERA
    Multiple (1965) *See Catalog Pages*

This "ordinary looking" camera turns into a deadly weapon in the hands of a ten year old! A highly collectible find.

Mint in Box $300-$350

**81. JAMES BOND ASTON-MARTIN
    (GOLD)**
    Corgi (1964) *Above*

Undoubtably the most famous 007 collectible of all. This first edition was issued in gold, along with a host of working features. Machine guns, bullet-proof windshield and, of course, ejector seat are included. The elaborate display box makes this item very valuable. (Corgi Catalog No. 261)

VG to Mint $300-$400

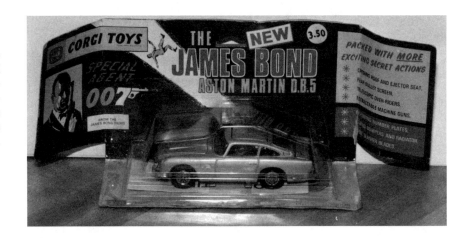

82. JAMES BOND ASTON-MARTIN (SILVER)
    Corgi (1966) *Above right*

Produced in the actual color of the film version, this DB5 has all the features of the gold car plus revolving front and rear license plates and tire slashers. (Corgi Catalog No. 270)

VG to Mint $225-$250

83. ASTON-MARTIN DB5 "HUSKY VERSION"
    Corgi (1968) *Not illustrated*

This is the first mini edition of the DB5, later to become known as "Corgi Juniors." The ejector seat is the only working feature of this car. (Corgi Catalog No. 1001)

Mint in Box $150-$175

84. TOYOTA GT 2000
 Corgi (1967)

From YOU ONLY LIVE TWICE, this
Bond car has figures of Aki and 007
accompanying it. As always, the Corgi
box is terrific. (Corgi Catalog No. 336)

Good to Mint $350-$400

*The following four Corgi vehicles were issued as part of the "Husky" line-up from ON HER MAJESTY'S SECRET SERVICE.
Each were packaged in a blister pack.*

85. ON HER MAJESTY'S SECRET SERVICE JAMES BOND S.P.E.C.T.R.E. MERCEDES
 Corgi (1969) *Not illustrated*

Mint on Blister Pack $200-$225

86. ON HER MAJESTY'S SECRET SERVICE MERCURY COUGAR
 Corgi (1969) *Not illustrated*

Mint on Blister Pack $200-$225

87. ON HER MAJESTY'S SECRET SERVICE BOND'S BOBSLED
 Corgi (1969) *Not illustrated* (Corgi Catalog No. 1011)

Mint on Blister Pack $200-$225

88. ON HER MAJESTY'S SECRET SERVICE BLOFELD'S BOBSLED
 Corgi (1969) *Not illustrated* (Corgi Catalog No. 1012)

Mint on Blister Pack $200-$225

89. JAMES BOND MUSTANG MACH I
 Corgi (1972) *Not illustrated*

This die-cast from DIAMONDS ARE FOREVER
(Tiffany Case's Mustang) has a rather plain box
design when compared to previous Corgi releases.
Still a somewhat rare item, this red Ford fastback is
a good find for any collector. (Corgi Catalog No.
391)

VG to Mint $250-$300

90. JAMES BOND 007 MOONBUGGY
 Corgi (1972) *Right*

Perhaps the best Bond die-cast ever made, also from
DIAMONDS ARE FOREVER.   A classic. (Corgi
Catalog No. 811)

VG to Mint $450-$475

91. JAMES BOND 007 ASTON-MARTIN
Corgi (1977)

Yet another edition of the DB5, this one does not have the revolving license plates or tire slashers. The Corgi catalog number for this version is #271, which was also used for an early 1980's issue. The 1977 car has a red interior; the 1980's car a cream interior.

1977 Issue $100 Mint in Box
1980's Issue $75 Mint in Box

92. WHIZZ-WHEELS CORGI JR. ASTON-MARTIN
Corgi (1972) *Not illustrated*

The "Whizz-Wheel" blister pack edition of the Junior DB5. (Corgi Catalog No. 1001/42)

Mint in Package $75

93. ASTON-MARTIN/LOTUS ESPRIT GIFT SET
Corgi (1977) *Not illustrated*

An overproduction of both vehicles prompted Corgi to issue this set, which included the Lotus Esprit from THE SPY WHO LOVED ME. (Corgi Catalog No. 2521)

Mint on Card $50-$75

94. CORGI JR. JAMES BOND GIFT SET
Corgi (1979) *Above*

This great "Junior's" set has one item not available separately. Included are Bond's Aston-Martin, Lotus Esprit, the Drax Helicopter and Space Shuttle. The ringer in the set is the rare "Jaws Van", giving a toothy price to this collectibles value.

VG to Mint $150-$175

95. ASTON-MARTIN CORGI JR.
Corgi (1979) *Not illustrated*

One more release of the small DB5, this time on a photo bubble pack.

Mint $30-$40

96. JAMES BOND LOTUS ESPRIT
Corgi (1977) *Right*

THE SPY WHO LOVED ME Bond car comes in a box with nice graphics and a plastic window. Trunk rockets, side fins (with recessed wheels) and periscope. This vehicle is worthy of addition to your Bond collection.

Mint in Box $100

97. LOTUS ESPRIT CORGI JR.
Corgi (1977) *Below, right*

This smaller version was sold on a bubble card.

Mint on Card $50

98. LOTUS ESPRIT GIFT PACK
Corgi (1977) *Not illustrated*

This double-feature has both the big and small versions of the Lotus. (Corgi Catalog No. 1362)

Mint in Box $75-$100

99. STROMBERG HELICOPTER
Corgi (1977) *Not illustrated*

A somewhat plain-looking collectible from THE SPY WHO LOVED ME.

Mint in Box $75-$100

100. STROMBERG HELICOPTER CORGI JR.
Corgi (1977) *Right*

This mini-version of the copter was also available from Corgi.

Mint on Card $25

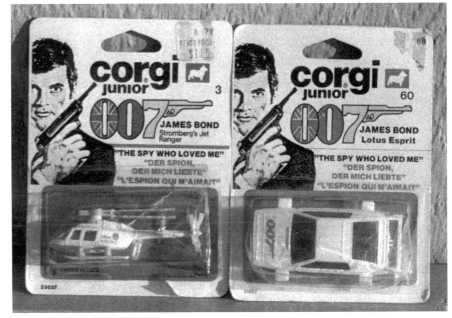

101. ASTON-MARTIN GIFT PACK
Corgi (1978) *Not illustrated*

Includes large and small editions of Bond's DB-5.

Mint in Box $75-$100

102. CORGI GIFT PACK #22
Corgi (1979) *Not illustrated*

This rare set has the large editions of the Drax Space Shuttle, the Aston Martin DB-5, the Lotus Esprit and the MOONRAKER satellite.

Mint in Box $150-$200

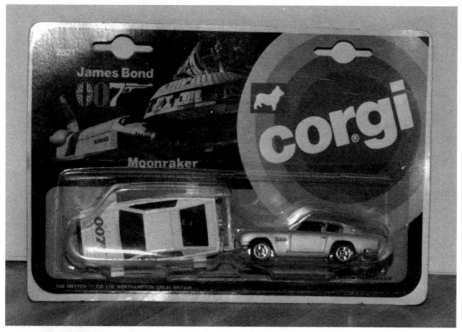

103. MOONRAKER CORGI JR. SET
    Corgi (1979) *Above*

Although neither the Aston-Martin or the Lotus Esprit appear in MOONRAKER, they do appear in this set.

Mint on Card $40-$50

104. SPY WHO LOVED ME JR. SET
    Corgi (1977) *Not illustrated*

This set packaged the Junior versions of the Lotus Esprit and the Drax Helicopter on a large cardboard blister pack.

Mint on Card $50

105. MOONRAKER DRAX HELICOPTER
    Corgi (1979) *Not illustrated* (Corgi Catalog No. 930)

A re-packaging of the Stromberg chopper, albeit in an attractive box.

Mint in Box $75-$95

106. MOONRAKER SPACE SHUTTLE
    Corgi (1979) *Below* (Corgi Catalog No. 649)

A large white space shuttle, trimmed in black with a Drax emblem, make this an attractive collectible.

VG to Mint in Box $75-$100

107. MOONRAKER JR. HELICOPTER
Corgi (1979) *Not illustrated*

This tiny Drax Helicopter came in a blister pack.

Mint on Card $25

108. MOONRAKER JR. SHUTTLE
Corgi (1977) *Not illustrated*

Another petite version, in a a small blister pack.

Mint on Card $25

109. MOONRAKER SHUTTLE AND COPTER JR. SET
Corgi (1979) *Not illustrated*

A re-packaging of the Stromberg chopper, albeit in an attractive box.

Mint in Box $75-$95

110. FOR YOUR EYES ONLY CITROEN
Corgi (1981) *Not illustrated*

This somewhat un-Bondian vehicle was offered smartly window-boxed and painted yellow. (Corgi Catalog No. 272)

Mint in Box $75-$100

111. CITROEN CORGI JUNIOR
Corgi (1981) *Not illustrated*

Smaller version of above.

Mint on Card $25

112. OCTOPUSSY GIFT SET
Corgi (1983) *Right, top* (Corgi Catalog No. E-3019)

A large blister pack set includes the Acrostar jet plane, plus the car and trailer from OCTOPUSSY.

Mint on Card $75-$100

113. A VIEW TO A KILL TAXI
Matchbox (1985) *Middle, right*

Poster art from the film is featured on the box of this Junior-sized die-cast.

Mint in Box $25-$30

114. A VIEW TO A KILL ROLLS-ROYCE
Matchbox (1985) *Middle, left*

This car includes the same box art as the taxi, above.

Mint in Box $25-$30

115. LICENSE TO KILL GIFT SET
Matchbox (1989) *Right, bottom*

One of the best die-cast sets ever produced, from the box art to the quality of the vehicles themselves. Includes the Jeep, seaplane, oil tanker and helicopter from LICENSE TO KILL. Sure to increase in value.

Mint in Box $75-$100

116. JAMES BOND 007 ASTON-MARTIN
   Corgi (1988) *Above*

Another re-release of this popular collector's item. This version comes in a plastic-topped box with a "007 Badge" included. (Corgi Catalog No. 94060)

Mint in Box $40

117. JAMES BOND 007 ASTON-MARTIN
   Corgi (1992) *Below*

After a three year absence from the marketplace, the DB-5 reappeared in a Swiss alpine backdrop box. (Also cataloged as Corgi Catalog No. 94060)

Mint in Box $40

118. 30TH ANNIVERSARY 007 ASTON-MARTIN
   Corgi (1992) *Not illustrated*

An exact replica of the original DB-5 release, right down to the gold plating. Only 7,500 of these were produced, each having a numbered certificate. Already a pricey item, these are sure to rise in value. (Corgi Catalog No. 96445)

Mint in Box $150-$200

119. GOLDENEYE ASTON-MARTIN
Corgi (1995) *Right, top*

Nice artwork of Pierce Brosnan on the front, along with good graphics of 007 and Isabella Scorupco on the back. (Corgi Catalog No. 96657)

Mint in Box $30-$40

120. GOLDENEYE RED FERRARI 355
Corgi (1995) *Right, middle*

The Xenia Onatopp Ferrari is graced with the same box as the GOLDENEYE Aston-Martin above. (Corgi Catalog No. 92978)

Mint in Box $30-$40

121. JAMES BOND ASTON -MARTIN DB-5
Corgi (1995) *Below*

This is a re-release of the fully functional 1966 Aston-Martin, even including the original packaging. Sure to rise in value. (Corgi Catalog No. 96655)

Mint in Box $25-$40

122. GOLDENEYE BLUE BMW Z3
Minichamps (1996) *Right, bottom*

The BMW comes in special GOLDENEYE packaging.

Mint in Box $40

123. LIVE AND LET DIE VIEWMASTER SET
  GAF (1973) *Left, top*

Three reels of 3-D pictures taken on the set of the the first Roger Moore Bond film. Came with a storybook tucked inside.

Mint in Package $40-$50

124. MOONRAKER VIEWMASTER SET
  GAF (1979) *Left, bottom*

"Moore" 3-D adventures, this time from MOONRAKER.

Mint in Package $20-$30

125. JAMES BOND 007 TAROT CARDS
  V.S. Game Systems (1973) *Right*

Just like the ones seen in LIVE AND LET DIE, these large cards have beautiful color artwork. The box is a bright yellow, with graphics from the film.

Mint in Box $40-$50

126. LIVE AND LET DIE PROMO BAG
  Glastron (1973) *Not illustrated*

A tie-in with Glastron boats, which were used in the filming of the movie, the bag has neat graphics on both sides.

Mint $30-$40

127. JAMES BOND WRISTWATCH RADIO
  Vanity Fair (1978) *Not illustrated*

A timely collectible, with an up-to-date value.

Mint in Package $50-$75

128. JAMES BOND 007 PINBALL MACHINE
  Gottlieb (1979) *Not illustrated*

This incredible James Bond collectible has great graphics of Roger Moore as 007, a bevy of beautiful women and, of course, "Jaws."

VG to Mint $5,000-$6,000

129. THE SPY WHO LOVED ME JIGSAW PUZZLE
H.G. Toys (1977) *Left, top*

A 150-piece puzzle, in a colorful box with unique graphics of Bond vs. Jaws.

Mint in Box $40-$50

130. THE SPY WHO LOVED ME JIGSAW PUZZLE
H.G. Toys (1977) *Left, middle*

A 150-piece puzzle, in a colorful box with unique graphics of Bond, Jaws and Anya with helicopter.

Mint in Box $40-$50

131. THE SPY WHO LOVED ME JIGSAW PUZZLE
H.G. Toys (1977) *Left, bottom*

A 150-piece puzzle, in a colorful box with unique graphics of Bond fighting with Jaws beside the Lotus Esprit.

Mint in Box $40-$50

132. JAMES BOND MOONRAKER DELUXE FIGURE
    Mego (1979) *Not illustrated*

This 12-inch doll came in an oversized box and included many accessories.

Mint in Box $550-$600

133. JAMES BOND MOONRAKER DOLL
    Mego (1979) *Right*

This version came in a smaller box and included just a spacesuit. A more down to earth collectible.

Mint in Box $125-$150

134. HOLLY GOODHEAD MOONRAKER DOLL
    Mego (1979) *Not illustrated*

Just as with the above doll, this one comes with a spacesuit. It's a little rarer and therefore a little more valuable.

Mint in Box $150-$175

135. HUGO DRAX MOONRAKER DOLL
    Mego (1979) *Not illustrated*

MOONRAKER's bad-guy doll brings a slight premium too.

Mint in Box $150-$175

136. JAWS MOONRAKER DOLL
    Mego (1979) *Not illustrated*

The rarest of the MOONRAKER quartet, this steel-toothed outlaw is a prized collectible.

Mint in Box $500-$600

137. JAMES BOND MOONRAKER
       HALLOWEEN COSTUME
    Ben Cooper (1979) *Not illustrated*

The only thing scary about this MOONRAKER spacesuit costume, which included a mask featuring Roger Moore's face, is its current value.

Mint in Box $60-$80

138. MOONRAKER TRADING CARDS
Topps (1979) *Left and below*

The complete set includes 90 cards. Each pack came with wrapper and stickers.

Complete Card Set; Mint $50-$60
Display Box; VG to Mint $20-$25

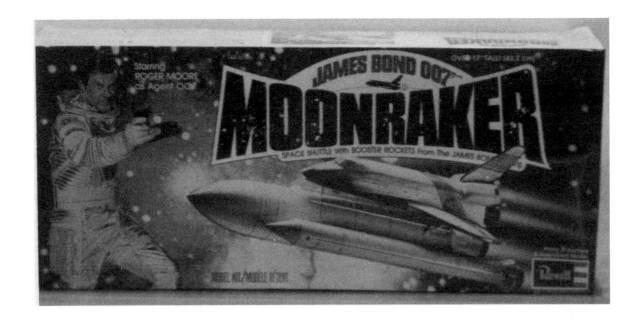

139. MOONRAKER SPACE SHUTTLE KIT
Revell (1979) *Above*

An all-plastic assembly kit that came in both a large and small version.

Deluxe Edition; Mint in Box $150-$175
Junior Edition; Mint in Box $20-$25

140. MOONRAKER SPACE SHUTTLE KIT
Airfix (1979) *Not illustrated*

Virtually identical to the Revell kit, but much rarer.

Mint in Box $100-$125

141. JAMES BOND 007 WALL CLOCK
Manufacturer unknown (1981) *Not illustrated*

A painting of Roger Moore is the on the face of this large time piece.

Mint in Box $70-$80

142. FOR YOUR EYES ONLY JAMES BOND AUTOMATIC 100 GUN
Crescent (1982) *Not illustrated*

This die-cast gun comes in an attractive box showing Roger Moore brandishing the weapon.

Mint in Package $200-$250

143. OCTOPUSSY JAMES BOND SPIN-SAW
Playcraft (1983) *Not illustrated*

This is the "yo-yo saw" seen in the film. A sharp toy!

Mint in Package $25-$30

144. OCTOPUSSY T.V. WATCH
   Seiko (1983) *Not illustrated*

An exact duplicate of 007's wristwatch from the OCTOPUSSY, with a working T.V. A high priced item when new, it originally sold for $495. Includes color flyer.

Mint in Box $600-$650

145. OCTOPUSSY "ALL TIME HIGH" 45 RPM RECORD WITH PICTURE SLEEVE
   A&M Records (1983) *Below*

A photograph of Rita Coolidge, plus poster artwork from the film make this a nice display piece.

Mint $15-$20

The following three items manufactured by Imperial, each came in a photo blister-pack with a picture of Roger Moore:

146. JAMES BOND 007 DART GUN
   Imperial (1984) *Not illustrated*

Mint in Package $20-$30

147. JAMES BOND 007 SUBMACHINE GUN
   Imperial (1984) *Not illustrated*

Mint in Package $20-$30

148. JAMES BOND 007 .380 PISTOL
   Imperial (1984) *Not illustrated*

Mint in Package $20-$30

149. JAMES BOND 007 WRISTWATCH
  Imperial (1984) *Not illustrated*

Sold in a blister-pack with a picture of Roger Moore. This item has a light-up dial.

Mint in Package $30-$40

150. JAMES BOND 007 SUNGLASSES
  Imperial (1984) *Not illustrated*

Cool shades suited for any 10-year old spy.

Mint on Card $30-$35

151. JAMES BOND PARACHUTE SET
  Imperial (1984) *Not illustrated*

A figure with an orange and green parachute comes in this bubble card pack.

Mint on Card $15-$25

152. JAMES BOND 007 DOG TAGS
  Imperial (1984) *Not illustrated*

Did 007 really wear these?

Mint on Card $5-$10

153. JAMES BOND 007 WALKIE-TALKIE
  Imperial (1984) *Not illustrated*

Another imperially priced item.

Mint in Box $15-$20

154. JAMES BOND I.D. TAGS
  Imperial (1984) *Not illustrated*

A great luggage tag for your exploding briefcase.

Mint on Card $10-$15

155. JAMES BOND "MAYDAY" PISTOL
  Coibel (1985) *Not illustrated*

A VIEW TO A KILL tie-in, this is a 12-shot toy armament.

Mint on Card $40-$50

156. JAMES BOND TWIN BELL ALARM CLOCK
    Zeon (1984) *Not illustrated*

A picture of Roger Moore is on the clock face of this item.

Mint in Box $50-$60

157. 007 STING PISTOL
    Coibel (1984) *Not illustrated*

An eight-shot cap pistol, plus a book from ON HER MAJESTY'S SECRET SERVICE are included.

Mint on Card $30-$40

158. 007 HIDEAWAY PISTOL
    Coibel (1984) *Not illustrated*

A neat trick pistol.

Mint on Card $30-$40

159. 007 EXPLODING CIGARETTE LIGHTER
    Coibel (1984) *Not illustrated*

Mint on Card $15-$20

160. 007 EXPLODING COIN
    Coibel (1984) *Not illustrated*

Mint on Card $15-$20

161. 007 EXPLODING PEN
    Coibel (1984) *Not illustrated*

Mint on Card $15-$20

162. 007 EXPLODING SPOON
    Coibel (1984) *Not illustrated*

Mint on Card $15-$20

163. JAMES BOND 007 SECRET SPY SET
    Coibel (1985) *Not illustrated*

This deluxe Coibel collectible features a pistol, shoulder holster, the exploding coin, spoon and pen. A hideaway gun with ankle holster, wallet and more are also included.

Mint in Box $150-$200

164. JAMES BOND THUNDERBALL PISTOL
     Coibel (1985) *Not illustrated*

A passport comes packed with this gun.

Mint in Package $25-$30

165. JAMES BOND POP UP TARGET SET
     Coibel (1985) *See Catalog Pages*

The rarest of the Coibel-manufactured items, this large-size set has a gun, darts and targets of the villians.

Mint in Box $125-$150

166. A VIEW TO A KILL 45 RPM RECORD
     Capitol (1985) *Not illustrated*

The picture-sleeve version of the Duran-Duran title song has a nice photo cover featuring Roger Moore.

Mint in Sleeve $15-$20

167. A VIEW TO A KILL MICHELIN BUTTON
A comnmercial promo tie-in, this large pin-back button shows 007 with the Michelin Man.

Mint $10-$12

168. CRUNCH 'N MUNCH CEREAL BOX
     General Foods (1985) *Not illustrated*

Another cross-promotion, this snack box has VIEW TO A KILL illustrations withb contest entry forms.

Mint Unopened Box $30-$35

169. VIEW TO A KILL HARDBACK STORY BOOK
     Grosset & Dunlap (1985) *Not illustrated*

Many rare photos are included in this nice storybook of the film.

Mint $10-$15

170. JAMES BOND "MAYDAY" PISTOL
     Coibel (1985) *Not illustrated*

A VIEW TO A KILL tie-in, this is a 12-shot toy armament.

Mint on Card $40-$50

171. JAMES BOND DRINKING GLASSES
Manufacturer unknown (1985) *Left*

This set of four unique drinking glasses were given away as Popeye's Restaurant promotion. THE SPY WHO LOVED ME, MOONRAKER, FOR YOUR EYES ONLY and A VIEW TO A KILL are featured.

Individual glasses; Mint $15-$20
Complete Set; Mint $60-$80

172. THE STORY OF JAMES BOND STICKER BOOK
Dajaq (1985) *Not illustrated*

This item came with 100 various stickers covering all the films from DR. NO through A VIEW TO A KILL. Today, the collectible has a high price sticker!

Mint $50-$60

173. JAMES BOND ASTON-MARTIN
Danbury Mint (1987) *Not illustrated*

A beautiful Corgi-sized replica of the Aston-Martin DB-5. The car is painted in a brilliant silver and comes with a wooden display base. A real collectible.

Mint $500-$600

174. JAMES BOND ASTON-MARTIN REPLICA
Danbury Mint (1997) *Not illustrated*

A 1:24 scale model of Bond's famous car. Authentically detailed, 7 1/4" in length, this model has over 300 parts. According to an advertisement, "Nothing can prepare you for the incredible number of working parts on this spectacular replica. The ejector seat actually blasts through the roof, the bullet-proof shield inside the trunk pops up, both license plates rotate, a tire slasher slides out of the left rear wheel hub and working 'rams' can actually be pulled out of both the front and rear bumpers." Originally offered for sale at $149.

Mint $300

175. JAMES BOND ROLE PLAYING GAMES
   Victory (1985-1987) *Right*

These games were loosely based on the films and permitted the average guy to be a super-sleuth, albeit in the safe environs of his living room. Each box depicts a scene from the movie, but Bond's appearance has been altered to a generic figure.

The following sets were available:

BASIC SET
Q'S MANUAL
GAME MASTER PACK
BOND VILLIANS
ASSAULT SET
DR. NO
GOLDFINGER
GOLDFINGER II
YOU ONLY LIVE TWICE
LIVE AND LET DIE
MAN WITH THE GOLDEN GUN
MAN WITH THE GOLDEN GUN II
OCTOPUSSY
A VIEW TO A KILL

Mint and Sealed in Box $15-$20

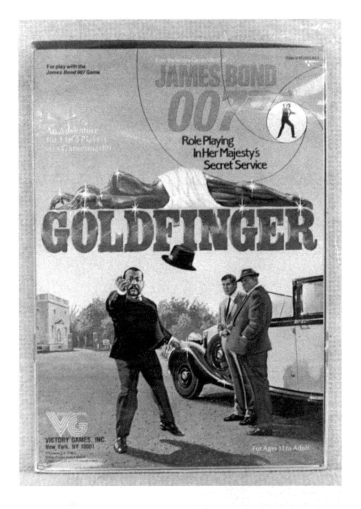

176. "THE LIVING DAYLIGHTS" TITLE SONG 45 RPM RECORD
   Warner Bros. Records (1987) *Not illustrated*

This version of the A-Ha title tune has a photo sleeve.

Mint with Sleeve $15-$20

177. "IF THERE WAS A MAN" 45 RPM RECORD
   Warner Bros. Records (1987) *Below*

Also from THE LIVING DAYLIGHTS soundtrack, this Pretenders song has a great photo sleeve of Timothy Dalton and Maryam D'Abo. This photo sleeve single would be the last to be produced as 45 rpm records began falling out of favor with buyers.

Mint with Sleeve $15-$20

178. 007 BULLET HOLE STICKERS
   CMP (1987) *Not illustrated*

These simulated bullet holes were designed to mount on a car's windshield, and surely looked best on an Aston-Martin. Also included was a magnetic license holder.

Mint in Package $15-$25

179. JAMES BOND CHESS SET
   Little Lead Soldiers (1987) *Not illustrated*

A very small number of these sets were produced, making this quite a valuable collectible today. The playing board doubles as a storage case and the chess pieces are made up of one-inch hand-painted figures of 007, his allies, his women and assorted villians.

Mint $450-$500

180. JAMES BOND ASTON-MARTIN KIT
Little Lead Soldiers (1987) *Not illustrated*

Another extremely rare item, the Corgi-sized kit comes unassembled in a nice gift box.

Mint in Box $200-$250

181. JAMES BOND PEN
Little Lead Soildiers (1987) *Not illustrated*

This collectible comes on a sealed blister-pack.

Mint on Card $10-$15

182. BOND FIGURINE AND GIFT CARD
Little Lead Soldiers (1987) *Not illustrated*

Handpainted one-inch figuremounted on an attractive card.

Mint $10-$15

183. JAMES BOND FIGURINE SETS
Little Lead Soldiers (1987) *Not illustrated*

Fantastically detailed, the handpainted one-inch figures came in three sets each packaged in a red velvet backing with the "007" logo.

Set #1   BOND AND HIS TEAM
Set #2   BOND AND HIS GIRLS
Set #3   BOND VILLIANS

Each Set, in Mint Condition $50-$60

184. HAPPY ANNIVERSARY 007 VIDEOTAPE
CBS-Fox Video (1987) *Right*

This 25th anniversary video is hosted by Roger Moore and has an emphasis on the latest Bond film at the time, THE LIVING DAYLIGHTS.

Mint, Sealed Tape $30-$40

185. "NEVER SAY NEVER AGAIN" TITLE SONG 45 RPM RECORD
    A&M Records (1983) *Below*

One of the few collectibles from NEVER SAY NEVER AGAIN. The disc's sleeve shows singer Lani Hall (who's married to A&M Records' founder Herb Alpert) in front of a photo of Sean Connery from the film.

Mint $15-$20

186. LICENSE TO KILL COMPUTER GAME
    Commodore (1989) *Not illustrated*

This computer game came packed in a box with great graphics and artwork. But the real collectible would be a Commodore computer to play the game with!

Mint in Box $25

187. JAMES BOND COMPUTER GAME
    IBM/Tandy (1990) *Not illustrated*

"The Stealth Affair" is loosely based on LICENSE TO KILL. Another artistically designed package.

Good to Mint in Box $25-$30

188. LICENSE TO KILL COMIC BOOK
    Eclipse (1989) *Not illustrated*

An illustrated version of the film with a color photo of Timothy Dalton on the cover. Makes an affordable collectible.

VG to Mint $5-$10

189. LICENSE TO KILL SATIN BANNER
    Manufacturer unknown (1989) *Not illustrated*

This giant display has a wonderful scene of Timothy Dalton as Bond in action.

VG to Mint $50-$60

190. JAMES BOND 007 CALENDAR
Manufacturer unknown (1991) *Not illustrated*

An over-sized calendar with various Bond scenes for each month. The cover features Timothy Dalton and Carey Lowell from LICENSE TO KILL.

Mint $15-$20

191. JAMES BOND TRADING CARDS
SET #1
Eclipse (1992) *Right, top*

This first set includes DR. NO, FROM RUSSIA WITH LOVE, GOLFDFINGER and THUNDERBALL. Neat holograms of Oddjob and the Aston-Martin contribute to this collectible's value.

Mint $50-$60

192. JAMES BOND TRADING CARDS
SET #2
Eclipse (1993) *Right, bottom*

YOU ONLY LIVE TWICE, ON HER MAJESTY'S SECRTET SERVICE, DIAMONDS ARE FOREVER and LIVE AND LET DIE make up this second set of cards. Includes a six-card subset of the Bond girls.

Mint $40-$50

193. JAMES BOND TRADING CARD BINDER
Eclipse (1992) *Not illustrated*

A notebook-sized card holder is a nice addition to the above sets.

Mint $10-$15

194. ASTON-MARTIN MODEL KIT
Doyusha (1994) *Left, top*

An extremely attractive box and kit. Also
includes figures of Bond and Oddjob. Sure
to rise in value.

Mint $45-$65

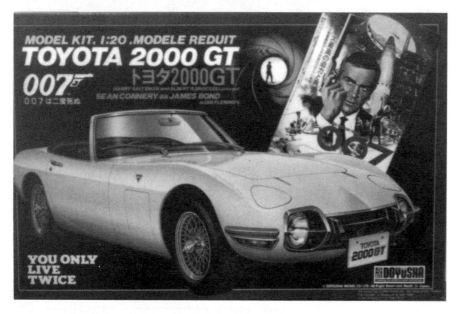

195. TOYOTA 2000GT MODEL KIT
Doyusha (1995) *Left, center*

Another great collectible from Doyushu.
This sports car from YOU ONLY LIVE
TWICE comes with figures of Bond and
Aki.

Mint $45-$65

196. MOONRAKER SHUTTLE KIT
Doyusha (1996) *Not illustrated*

James Bond, Jaws and Holly Goodhead figures all come with this scale model of the
space shuttle from MOONRAKER.

Mint $40-$50

**197. JAMES BOND 007
MICRO-MACHINES**
Galoob (1995) *Left, bottom*

Miniature figures and vehicles from
GOLDFINGER, THE SPY WHO LOVED
ME and MOONRAKER are included in this
nice boxed set.

Mint $15-$20

198. GOLDENEYE CALENDAR
Landmark (1995) *Not illustrated*

Twelve photos from the 007 adventure are featured on this collectible.

Mint $10-$15

199. GOLDENEYE TRADING CARDS
Graffiti (1995) *Right, top and bottom*

This card set is devoted entirely to scenes from GOLDENEYE and includes several sub-set cards (below).

Mint Complete Set $50-$60

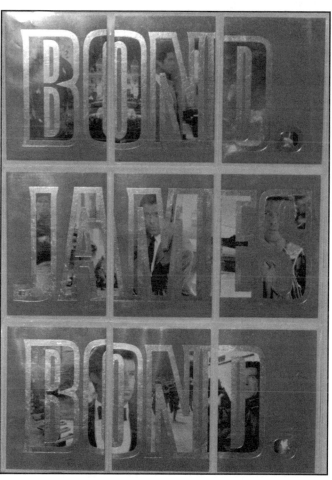

200. GOLDENEYE SATELLITE CLOCK
   Manufacturer unknown (1995) *Above*

The GOLDENEYE logo graces the front of this sleek clock.

Mint with Box $10-$15

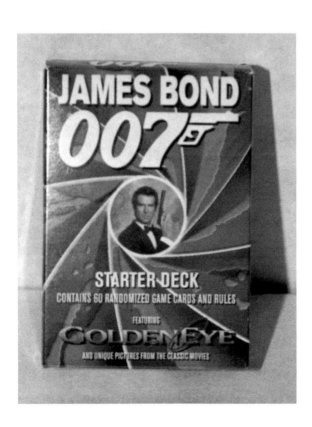

201. GOLDENEYE CARD GAME
   Target Games (1995) *Left*

This game pits 007 against variuous plots and includes 67 "Common Cards", 69 "Uncommon Cards", 64 "Rare Cards" and ten "Chase Cards" for a complete set. A starter deck comes with 60 randomly packed cards with 15-card booster packs availably separately.

Starter Deck, Mint $10-$12
Booster Sets, Mint $4-$5

202. GOLDENEYE CD SINGLE
   Virgin (1995) *Not illustrated*

The 90's version of a 45 RPM picture sleeve. Tina Turner sings the title song along with several twists on the theme.

Mint $5-$10

203. GOLDENEYE SUNCOAST PHONECARD
GTI Telephone (1995) *Right*

A truly different promotional tie-in, this card was only available at Suncoast Video Stores. The package also included coupons for discounts on various Bond items.

Mint, unopened $8-$10

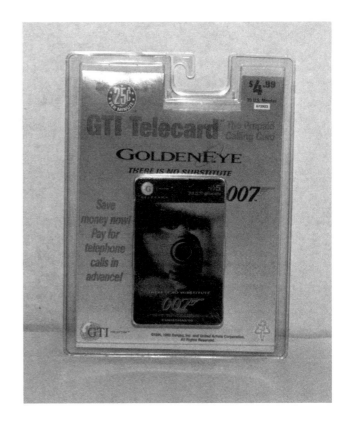

204. GOLDENEYE LITE WATCH
Manufacturer unknown (1995) *Not illustrated*

This well made item comes with a black leather band, stainless steel casing and rotating bezel. The watch's face is black with both GOLDENEYE and United Artists logos.

Mint in Case $70-$80

205. JAMES BOND 007 MARTINI GLASS
Manufacturer unknown (1995) *Not illustrated*

A frosted GOLDENEYE logo is imprinted on these unique glasses.

Mint $12-$15

206. JAMES BOND MUGS
Manufacturer unknown (1995) *Not illustrated*

This collectible, marketed through MGM/UA during the initial release of GOLDENEYE, came in two different varieties: the GOLDENEYE logo in gold over black or the 007 logo in silver over black.

Mint $8-$10

207. ON HER MAJESTY'S SECRET SERVICE GIFT SET
Corgi (1969) *Not illustrated*

An extremely rare three vehicle set (Corgi Catalog No. 3004), it has both the Bond and Blofeld bobsleds as well as a VW Beetle!

VG to Mint $125-$150

208. CRIMEBUSTERS GIFT SET
Corgi (1969) *Not illustrated*

This Junior boxed gift set combines the Junior Aston-Martin with the Batmobile, Batboat and the MAN FROM U.N.C.L.E. blue missile-firing car. (Corgi Catalog No. 3005)

VG to Mint $75-$100

209. SPECIAL EDITION ASTON-MARTIN
Corgi (1995) *Not illustrated*

A special edition from Corgi; a re-issue of the original gold-plated DB-5.

Mint $30-$40

The Colgate-Palmolive Company participated in a major product tie-in during the initial 1965 release of THUNDERBALL. Numerous toiletry items targeted to men and boys were offered, all carrying the official James Bond 007 logo. However, by 1967 the line had been discontinued. These collectibles, when found today, are quickly increasing in value.

210.	**JAMES BOND 007 AFTERSHAVE**	*VG to Mint*	*$40-$50*
211.	**JAMES BOND 007 COLOGNE**	*VG to Mint*	*$40-$50*
212.	**JAMES BOND 007 SHAVING CREAM**	*VG to Mint*	*$40-$50*
213.	**JAMES BOND 007 SOAP (IN BOX)**	*VG to Mint*	*$40-$50*
214.	**JAMES BOND 007 TALC**	*VG to Mint*	*$40-$50*
215.	**JAMES BOND 007 HAIR DRESSING**	*VG to Mint*	*$40-$50*
216.	**JAMES BOND 007 PRE-ELECTRIC SHAVE LOTION**	*VG to Mint*	*$40-$50*
217.	**JAMES BOND 007 HAIR TONIC**	*VG to Mint*	*$40-$50*
218.	**JAMES BOND 007 GIFT SET**	*VG to Mint*	*$125-$150*

Included Talc and Aftershave

219.	**JAMES BOND 007 GIFT SET**	*VG to Mint*	*$125-$150*

Included Cologne and Aftershave

220.	**JAMES BOND 007 DELUXE GIFT SET**	*VG to Mint*	*$400-$500*

Included Shaving Cream, Soap, Talc, Deodorant, Aftershave Lotion, Cologne and Hair Tonic.
Came in a large gift box with the 007 logo.

221.	**JAMES BOND 007 GIFT SET**	*VG to Mint*	*$300-$350*

Included Cologne, Aftershave Lotion, Deodorant, Shaving Cream and Talc in a gift box.

222.	**JAMES BOND 007 GIFT SET**	*VG to Mint*	*$125-$150*

Included Aftershave Lotion and Shaving Cream in a gift box.

223.	**JAMES BOND 007 GIFT SET**	*VG to Mint*	*$125-$150*

Included Aftershave Lotion and Pre-Electric Shave Lotion in a gift box.

COLGATE'S Campaign for Men's Toiletries includes Network TV, National Mags, Newspapers...and more

The Colgate Palmolive Company has tied in an entire line of "007" toiletries for men, including *cologne, after-shave lotion, shaving cream, deodorant, hair-dressing and talcum powder.* This line is NOT for kids ... and Colgate's ad-promo budget is being spent on men and the women who buy for them. Colgate is using ten top network television programs to kick-off the line's advertising as well as local "spot" buys. In the print media, ads will also appear in Life, Look, Saturday Evening Post and other major magazines. Newspaper schedules have been prepared for this national saturation. Colgate hasn't overlooked a thing. Get on the phone right now and make a lunch date with your local distributor for Colgate ... and work with him on displays and tie-ins. He has all kinds of window streamers and point-of-purchase material, supplied by Colgate ... and will welcome whatever else you can offer. Offer anything he wants, from stills right up to the door-panels. This is a big national promotion ... but it's local size depends on you.

AFTER SHAVE

For further information, contact:

JAMES BOND MOVIE TIE-IN BOOKS

The James Bond novels by Ian Fleming have been published hundreds of times over the years. However, with the exception of very rare hardcover first printings, it is the paperback movie editions with their exciting artwork that attract the most collector interest.

Some of the Bond films had numerous paper and hardback releases. As collectibles, they make terrific low cost acqusitions.

224.   DR. NO PAPERBACK BOOK
     Signet (1962) *Left*

The back cover has a nice still from the film, while the front has a blurb promoting the movie's release.

VG to Mint $5-$10

225.   FROM RUSSIA WITH LOVE PAPERBACK BOOK
     Signet (1963) *Left*

A great cover, with photos of Sean Connery and Daniella Bianchi on a red background.

VG to Mint $5-$10

226. GOLDFINGER PAPERBACK BOOK
    Signet (1964) *Right*

Nice cover art and the first paperback movie edition to use the film's poster art.

VG to Mint $5-$10

227. THUNDERBALL PAPERBACK BOOK
    Signet (1965) *Right*

Stunning artwork of Sean Connery and Company on the front cover, plus a black and white still of 007 in action on the back cover.

VG to Mint $5-$10

228. YOU ONLY LIVE TWICE PAPERBACK BOOK
    Signet (1965) *Not illustrated*

A simple blurb, "Now a Smash United Artists Film," is all this edition can boast.

VG to Mint $5-$8

229. CASINO ROYALE PAPERBACK BOOK
    Signet (1966) *Right*

This film was a non-Eon production. It's tie-in book had a cover with the psychedelically tattooed girl from the movie poster.

VG to Mint $4-$8

230. ON HER MAJESTY'S SECRET SERVICE PAPERBACK BOOK
Signet (1969) *Left*

A black and white photo of the 1969 James Bond, George Lazenby, graces the cover of this movie tie-in paperback.

VG to Mint $4-$8

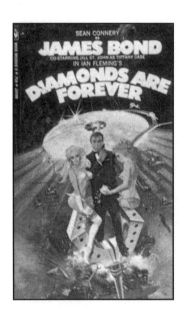

231. DIAMONDS ARE FOREVER PAPERBACK BOOK
Bantam (1971) *Left*

The terrific one-sheet artwork is used on the cover of this book. A hard cover Book Club Edition was also released, with an identical full color dust jacket.

Paperback: VG to Mint $5-$10
Hardcover Book Club Edition: VG to Mint $20-$25

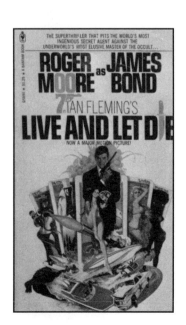

232. LIVE AND LET DIE PAPERBACK BOOK
Bantam (1973) *Left*

Another tie-in book which used the poster's great art.

VG to Mint $4-$8

**233. THE MAN WITH THE GOLDEN GUN
PAPERBACK BOOK**
Signet (1975) *Right, top*

A color photo of Roger Moore, Maud Adams and Britt Ekland appears on the front cover with a nice assortment of film scenes on the back cover.

VG to Mint $4-$8

234. THE SPY WHO LOVED ME PAPERBACK BOOK
Warner Books (1977) *Right, center*

A totally new novelization of the feature film written by Christopher Wood; not a Fleming book. The cover uses the one-sheet's artwork.

VG to Mint $4-$8

235. MOONRAKER PAPERBACK BOOK
Warner Books (1979) *Not illustrated*

Another novelization of the feature film. The cover also uses the poster's artwork.

VG to Mint $4-$8

236. FOR YOUR EYES ONLY COMIC BOOK
Marvel Comics (1981) *Not illustrated*

While no novel tie-ins were published for this film, Marvel Comics did release a comic-strip edition in full color.

VG to Mint $10-$15

237. LICENSE TO KILL HARDCOVER BOOK
Warner Books (1989) *Right, bottom*

The first 007 movie tie-in book release in ten years, this original novel by John Gardner has a nice color photo of Timothy Dalton on its cover. A hardcover Book Club Edition was also published using the film's teaser poster artwork.

Hardcover: VG to Mint $5-$10
Hardcover Book Club Edition: VG to Mint $10-$15

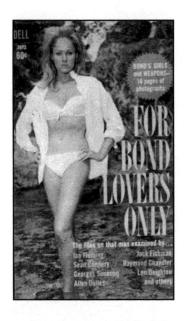

238. FOR BOND LOVERS ONLY PAPERBACK BOOK
Dell (1966) *Left, top*

This 1966 Dell book covers the Bond phenomenon up to that time. Profusely illustrated in a nice photo section.

VG to Mint $20-$25

239. GOLDENEYE PAPERBACK BOOK
Warner (1995) *Not illustrated*

Another John Gardner novelization adapted from the final film. This book has the promotional artwork of Pierce Brosnan on the cover.

VG to Mint $6-$8

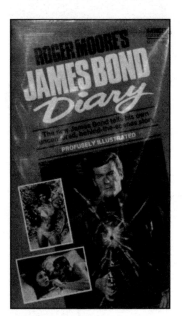

**240. ROGER MOORE'S JAMES BOND DIARY
PAPERBACK BOOK**
Fawcett (1973) *Left, center*

Printed in 1973 to coincide with the release of LIVE AND LET DIE, the cover has a nice photo of Roger Moore in his debut as 007. Although it is uncertain whether Moore actually wrote the book, it is good reading and really tells how a Bond film is made from beginning to end.

VG to Mint $5-$10

241. TOMORROW NEVER DIES PAPERBACK BOOK
Warner (1993) *Left, bottom*

The novelization of the movie by Raymond Benson based upon the screenplay by Bruce Feirstein. The book sports a cover with the film's promotional artwork.

VG to Mint $7-$8

REPRODUCTION PROPS FROM THE JAMES BOND FILMS

In 1995, S.D. Studios Ltd., through the James Bond Collector's Society, began to issue beautifully crafted reproductions of actual props used in the James Bond films. The pieces are limited in production. Each prop came in a walnut box with a glass lid emblazoned with the 007 logo, brass hardware and a combination lock pre-set to the code 0-0-7.

Other prop reproductions from S.D. Studios Ltd. include James Bond's attache case (with contents) from FROM RUSSIA WITH LOVE, Odd Job's steel-rimmed bowler hat from GOLDFINGER, the Walther P-99 from TOMORROW NEVER DIES, the 1934 Beretta from DR. NO and several other items. Included with each prop are stills and other rare information.

242. THE MAN WITH THE GOLDEN GUN GUN SET
   S.D. Studios Ltd. (1995) *Right; top*

This highly detailed collectible (non-working, of course) comes in its own case and is heavily plated in 24 carat gold. A golden engraved 007 bullet is included which can be loaded into the barrel. Disassembles into four parts.

Retail $675

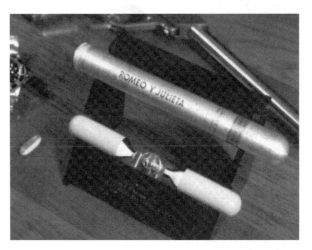

243. THUNDERBALL BREATHING DEVICE
   S.D. Studios Ltd. (1995) *Right; center*

Just like the one James Bond used to escape from Largo's shark-infested pool at Palmyra. A nicely boxed non-working prop, the center valve section is plated in 24 carat gold. Includes cigar case and display stand.

Retail $195

244. MOONRAKER WRIST DART GUN
   S.D. Studios Ltd. (1995) *Right; bottom*

A highly polished, machined aluminum gun, this neat prop from MOONRAKER comes with ten darts in a cassette carrying case. The gun has an adjustable wristband.

Retail $295

Photographs courtesy S.D. Studios Ltd.

JAMES BOND CRITERION LASER DISCS

Criterion, a manufacturer of high quality laser discs of digitally re-mastered motion pictures, released three special edition James Bond laser discs during 1990-1991.

Threatened by legal action over audio commentaries included on the discs by several Bond film-makers, the items were discontinued.

245. DR. NO LASERDISC
Criterion (1990) *Not illustrated*

Mint $200

246. FROM RUSSIA WITH LOVE LASERDISC
Criterion (1990) *Not illustrated*

Mint $200

247. GOLDFINGER LASERDISC
Criterion (1991) *Not illustrated*

Worth a bit more than the others, since it was on the market for such a short period of time.

Mint $250

248. JAMES BOND VIDEO GAME
Coleco (1983) *Not illustrated*

This home video cartridgecame in a box with standard Bond artwork. Finding a game machine to play it on might be more difficult than finding this collectible!

VG to Mint $25-$30

249. ON HER MAJESTY'S SECRET SERVICE FORD ESCORT
Corgi (1969) *Not illustrated*

An extremely rare item, this car is designed after one of the cars in the race sequence from ON HER MAJESTY'S SECRET SERVICE.

Mint on Card $200-$250

Vinyl albums featuring the soundtracxks from the James Bond films have always been popular. But with the advent of compact discs, and their subsequently tiny artwork, these frameable giants have become great collectibles.

The prices below reflect values based on Good to Mint copies. Some of the earlier soundtracks were released in both Mono and Stereo versions, but value differences between the two are negligible.

250. DR. NO RECORD ALBUM
United Artists (1963) *Right, top*

Originally issued in both Mono and Stereo, the black United Artists label was stamped onto the first release.

Good to Mint $35-$40

251. FROM RUSSIA WITH LOVE RECORD ALBUM
United Artists (1964) *Not illustrated*

Also a Stereo/Mono release, the main title theme was re-recorded, minus the organ as in the film version. The cuts "The Golden Horn", "Guitar Lament" and "Leila Dances" are not heard in the film, however.

Good to Mint $25-$30

252. GOLDFINGER RECORD ALBUM
United Artists (1964) *Right, bottom*

A black label Stereo/Mono release, this was the first Bond soundtrack to be a million seller. The "Goldfinger Instrumental" was originally released in stereo, but in mono on later pressings.

Good to Mint $25-$30

253. GOLDFINGER RECORD ALBUM (BRITISH RELEASE)
Sunset (1964) *Left, top*

This is the version of GOLDFINGER released in Great Britain. Non-U.S. versions of albums often featured different artwork on their covers, as was the case with non-U.S. posters.

Good to Mint $25-$30

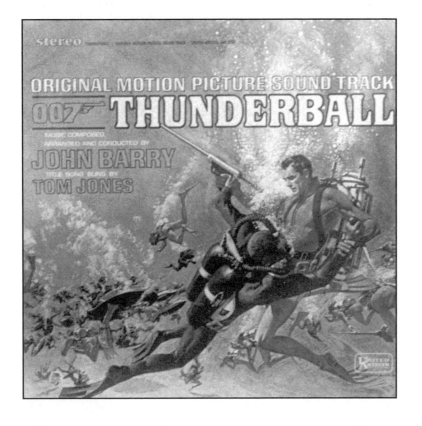

254. THUNDERBALL RECORD ALBUM
United Artists (1965) *Left, bottom*

A black label Stereo/Mono release, this album was over produced by United Artists Records in anticipation that the Tom Jones title song would make it a monster hit greater than GOLDFINGER. The versions of "Mr. Kiss-Kiss Bang-Bang" are different on the Mono and Stereo editions.

Good to Mint $15-$20

Exploitation

Campaign

In Albums, Singles, Tom Jones Vocal!

'Thunderball' Score

1. The fabulous score directly from the soundtrack of the picture has been pressed on a long-playing disc by United Artists Records. You remember what tremendous hits the albums of "Dr. No" and "From Russia With Love" were? Well, get ready for a repeat when the "Thunderball" score hits the stores and the airways—which is now!

2. Tom Jones, one of the country's top recording artists, sings "Thunderball" over the picture's titles and has also recorded it on the PARROT label (a London Records subsidiary). It is available at all record stores on a 45 rpm disc.

3. MGM Records has issued a single also—as well as 12" long-playing Album—recorded by "The Fantabulous Strings."

4. A host of other top label recordings which include:

Peter Nero — RCA Victor Records — Instrumental Single & Album
Billy Strange — Crescendo Records — Instrumental Single & Album
Hank Levine — Capitol Records — Instrumental Single & Album
Jazz Crusaders — Liberty Records — Instrumental Single & Album
Xavier Cugat — Decca Records — Instrumental Album
Jimmy Sedlar — Kapp Records — Instrumental Trumpet Single

Contact record dealers in your area and set up windows and point-of-sale displays. Bond is big business, as each distributor has been advised by record company home offices, and you will find dealers anxious to cooperate. If they are in shopping centers or department stores, where you have merchandise tied-in (see pages 2-5) involve these record dealers with whatever store-wide promotions you set. Plan a joint campaign with book and record dealers for cross displays wherever both items are sold. Offer records as well as books for door-prizes in contests and promotions.

Soundtrack
Album and
Tom Jones
Vocal

255. YOU ONLY LIVE TWICE   RECORD ALBUM
   United Artists (1967) *Not illustrated*

Another black United Artists label, this release was issued in both Mono and Stereo. One cut, "Tanaka's World," is not part of the final film's soundtrack.

Good to Mint $20-$25

256. CASINO ROYALE   RECORD ALBUM
   Colgems (1967) *Not illustrated*

This non Eon-produced Bond film's soundtrack was released by Colgems, a division of Columbia Pictures. Available in both Stereo and Mono, this is the rarest of the Bond vinyl soundtracks, though far from the best.

Good to Mint $40-$50

257. ON HER MAJESTY'S SECRET SERVICE   RECORD ALBUM
   United Artists (1969) *Not illustrated*

The first "Stereo Only" release of a Bond soundtrack, on United Artist's new orange and pink label. Only the Capitol Record Club editions were issued on the old black label, and are true rarities. It's cover was done exclusively for the album.

Good to Mint $20-$25

258. DIAMONDS ARE FOREVER   RECORD ALBUM
   United Artists (1971) *Not illustrated*

DIAMONDS ARE FOREVER marked the return of Sean Connery to Bond films and Shirley Bassey as the singer of the main title theme. Bassey had performed on a Bond soundtrack in 1964 with her smash version of GOLDFINGER. Released only in Stereo and on a new beige United Artists label.

Good to Mint $20-$25

259. MAN WITH THE GOLDEN GUN   RECORD ALBUM
   United Artists (1974) *Not illustrated*

This soundtrack album was the last to be released on United Artist's beige label. It is also the only Bond album to have the film's title logo on the disc label.

Good to Mint $15-$20

260. LIVE AND LET DIE RECORD ALBUM
United Artists (1973) *Right, top*

This Stereo release is the only Bond soundtrack to have
a lavish open-up gate folder (see below). This album
cost United Artists more to manufacture, but they must
have felt confident in sales with Paul McCartney and
Wings performing the main title theme. Nicely illustrated with color photos from the film, this release had
United Artists' beige label.

Good to Mint $25-$30

**261. THE SPY WHO LOVED ME
RECORD ALBUM**
United Artists (1977) *Right, bottom*

Released on the United Artist yellow and orange cloud
label, this album features totally re-recorded music performed especially for this album and therefore different
from the film score. The cut "Anya" is not included in
the final film.

Good to Mint $15-$20

262. MOONRAKER RECORD ALBUM
   United Artists (1979) *Not illustrated*

Released on the United Artist yellow and orange cloud label. Shirley Bassey was called back again to lend a classy sound to the main title theme.

Good to Mint $10-$15

263. FOR YOUR EYES ONLY RECORD ALBUM
   Liberty (1981) *Above*

A subsidiary of United Artists Records, Liberty Records, released this Bond soundtrack in 1981.

Good to Mint $10-$15

264. OCTOPUSSY RECORD ALBUM
   A&M Records (1983) *Not illustrated*

The demise of United Artists Records resulted in this soundtrack being release through A&M Records.

Good to Mint $10-$15

265. A VIEW TO A KILL RECORD ALBUM
   Capitol (1985) *Not illustrated*

Released on yet another new label, Capitol, this album marked the last film to feature Roger Moore as James Bond. But the really good news was that this would be the first Bond soundtrack album to be digitally recorded, making for brilliant sound.

Good to Mint $10-$15

266. THE LIVING DAYLIGHTS RECORD ALBUM
   Warner Bros. (1981) *Not illustrated*

A terrific vinyl soundtrack and, as of this writing, the last Bond score to be composed by John Barry. The soundtrack includes tunes by both The Pretenders and A-Ha.

Good to Mint $10-$15

**267. NEVER SAY NEVER AGAIN
RECORD ALBUM
(JAPANESE RELEASE)**
King Records (1983) *Right, top*

Surprisingly, no domestic U.S. release of this unique
Michel Legrand score was ever made. King Record
Company of Japan did distribute the soundtrack of this
non-Eon film overseas, making it a particularly valuable
find today.

Good to Mint $50-$75

**268. JAMES BOND 10TH ANNIVERSARY
RECORD ALBUM**
United Artists (1972) *Right, bottom*

A United Artists beige label release in 1972, this two-
record album has a nice open-up cover. The 'film strip'
artwork makes this album a great display piece.

Good to Mint $40-$50

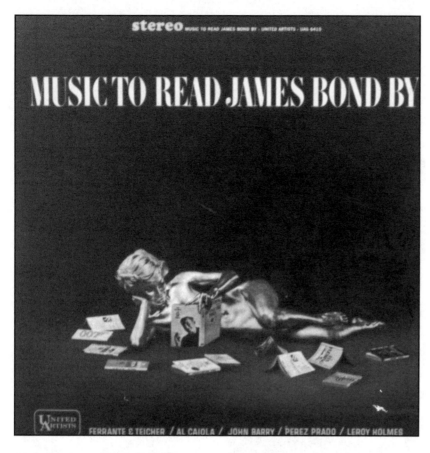

269. MUSIC TO READ JAMES BOND BY RECORD ALBUM
   United Artists (1967) *Above*

A 'Golden Girl' reading various James Bond novels provides the illustrative cover for the mix of original soundtrack cuts and new compositions by Leroy Holmes, Ferrante & Teicher, Al Caiola and Perez Prado. A Volume II of this album was also released, with the same collectible value.

Mint $25

270. THE INCREDIBLE WORLD OF JAMES BOND RECORD ALBUM
   United Artists (1965) *Not illustrated*

This 1965 compilation has two different album jackets, perhaps for different types of buyers. One has a pop-art illustration, the other a group of scantily clad women. Both have the same value.

Mint $20-$25

271. LICENSE TO KILL RECORD ALBUM
   Warner Bros. (1989) *Not illustrated*

The last vinyl album of a Bond soundtrack to be released, as compact discs took over the marketplace. With a score by Michael Kaman, the cover features poster art from the film.

Good to Mint $10-$15

272. OCTOPUSSY COMPACT DISC
   A&M Records (1997) *Not illustrated*

The long out-of-print OCTOPUSSY album was originally issued on compact disc by A&M Records in the mid-Eighties. This new release of the soundtrack is not only re-mastered, but includes a fold-out poster of the film's artwork, plus incidental dialogue and the film's trailer, which can be seen on a computer.

Mint $15

273. THE LIVING DAYLIGHTS COMPACT DISC
Warner Bros. (1998) *Not illustrated*

This second re-issue of THE LIVING DAYLIGHTS has been re-mastered with all the neat extras of the previously described OCTOPUSSY CD. A good future Bond collectible. This disc contains several unreleased tracks of great John Barry Bond music from the film.

Mint $15

274. JAMES BOND 30TH ANNIVERSARY LIMITED EDITION COMPACT DISC
United Artists (1992) *Below*

This future collectible, a two-CD set, is fantastic. The first disc features the title tunes to all the James Bond films from DR. NO through LICENSE TO KILL. The second disc is the real gem in this release, though. It contains previously unreleased music from THUNDERBALL and 'cover versions' of GOLDFINGER by Anthony Newley plus versions of YOU ONLY LIVE TWICE and MR KISS-KISS BANG-BANG by Shirley Bassey and Dionne Warwick.

Additionally, tracks from GOLDFINGER only issued in England are on Disc Two, as well as radio spots from THUNDER-BALL, YOU ONLY LIVE TWICE and LIVE AND LET DIE.

A single compact disc with just the cover tunes was also released at the same time.

Deluxe Edition; Mint $30
Abbreviated Edition; Mint $15

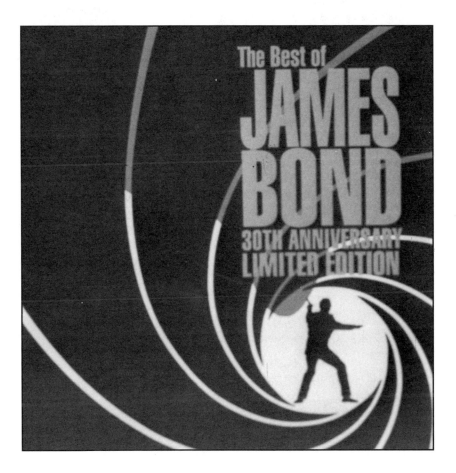

275.   JAMES BOND ACTION FIGURE DOLL #1
Gilbert (1964) *Top left and below; also see Catalog Pages*

This first issue doll, sold exclusively in the 1965 Sears Christmas Wishbook, differs from the second in apparel. A black or blue suit, white shirt and tie were packaged with this item. An extremely rare find. Only a few known to exist.

VG to Mint in Box $1,800-$2,000

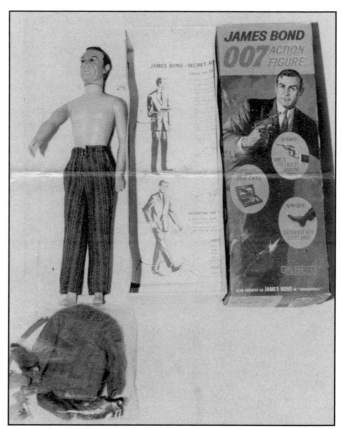

276.   JAMES BOND CONNOISSEUR CARDS
Inkworks (1996) *Opposite page; lower left*

A 90-card set covering the Bond films of the Sixties.

Basic Set   *Mint $20*
9-Card Subset "Women of Bond"   *Mint $45*
6-Card Subset "Bond Posters"   *Mint $60*
GOLD Bond Card   *Mint $40**
Unopened Box   *Mint $55*

* Note that a Platinum card from this set was mistakenly produced and included in the Volume 2 card set below. It's value is considerably higher than the Gold card.

277.   JAMES BOND CONNOISSEUR CARDS - VOLUME 2
Inkworks (1997) *Opposite page; top and lower right*

This second 90-card set, released a year later, features the Bond films of the Seventies.

Basic Set   *Mint $20*
9-Card Subset "Women of Bond"   *Mint $45*
5-Card Subset "Bond Posters"   *Mint $50*
GOLD Bond Card   *Mint $40*
Unopened Box   *Mint $55*

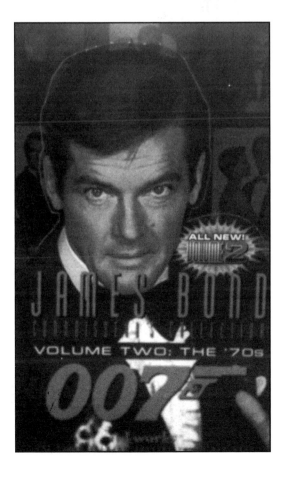

278. JAMES BOND CONNOISSEUR - VOLUME 3
Inkworks (1997) *Not illustrated*

The final 90-card set covers FOR YOUR EYES ONLY through GOLDENEYE.

Basic Set   *Mint $20*
9-Card Subset "Women of Bond"   *Mint $45*
6-Card Subset "Bond Posters"   *Mint $60*
GOLD Bond Card   *Mint $40*
Unopened Box   *Mint $55*

279. TOMORROW NEVER DIES CARD SET
Inkworks (1997) *Left, top and bottom*

Another 90-card set from Inkworks that also features two subsets, one of Teri Hatcher and three additional "Women of Bond" cards.

Basic Set   *Mint $20*
Teri Hatcher Subset   *Mint $45*
"Women of Bond" Subset   *Mint $30*

Left; top: Promo Card for TOMORROW NEVER DIES Card Set

Left; below: Box for TOMORROW NEVER DIES Card Set

280. JAMES BOND 1998 CALENDER
    TeNeves (1997) *Above*

A 12-month cornucopia of James Bond photos through
GOLDENEYE.

Mint Condition $12

281. TOMORROW NEVER DIES
    1998 CALENDAR
    TeNeves (1997) *Right, bottom*

This calender features 12 months worth of pictures from
TOMORROW NEVER DIES.

Mint Condition $12

282. GOLDENEYE VIDEO GAME
   Nintendo (1997) *Above*

A state-of-the-art video game designed exclusively for the Nintendo 64 Video Game System. This neat game allows the player to become 007 and live the 17th Bond adventure for themselves! Superb graphics and music make this a high quality and fun to use collectible.

Mint Condition $65

283. JAMES BOND ASTON-MARTIN DB5
      Corgi (1997) *Above*

Yet another re-issue of the Bond car in 1:43 scale, this Corgi comes in an attractive box along with a figure of Oddjob.

Mint in Box $40

284. TOMORROW NEVER DIES ASTON-MARTIN DB5
      Corgi (1997) *Not illustrated*

Released by Corgi to capitalize on TOMORROW NEVER DIES, the 18th Bond film, this 1:98 scale car is a good collectible at a good price.

Mint in Box $20

285. FOR YOUR EYES ONLY JAMES BOND 2CV CITROEN
      Solido (1997) *Not illustrated*

This 1:18 scale model of the chase car from FOR YOUR EYES ONLY comes in an attractive window box, and an attractive value.

Mint in Box $40

286. FOR YOUR EYES ONLY JAMES BOND 2CV CITROEN
      Vitesse (1997) *Not illustrated*

A limited edition in the real sense; only 2,000 were produced due to licensing problems.

Mint in Box $40

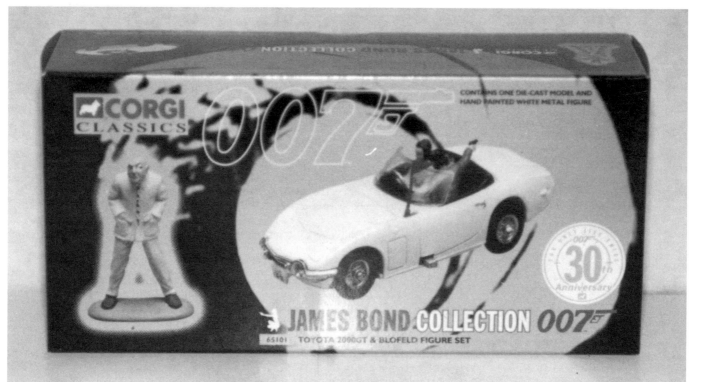

287. THE SPY WHO LOVED ME LOTUS ESPRIT
   Corgi (1997) *Opposite page; top*

A nicely boxed re-issue of the Lotus car-sub. This set includes a Jaws figurine.

Mint in Box $40

288. YOU ONLY LIVE TWICE TOYOTA 2000GT
   Corgi (1997) *Opposite page; bottom*

Released by Corgi on the 30th anniversary of the initial release of YOU ONLY LIVE TWICE. This car comes with a Blofeld figurine.

Mint in Box $40

289. DIAMONDS ARE FOREVER MOONBUGGY
   Corgi (1997) *Above*

This all-time collector favorite was re-issued by Corgi in 1997. The Moonbuggy comes with an extra 007 figurine.

Mint in Box $40

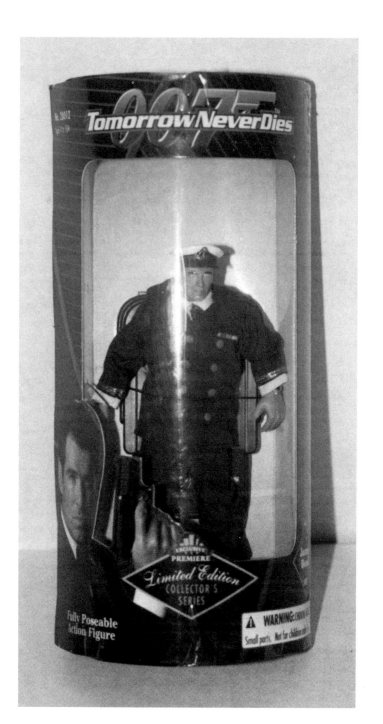

290. TOMORROW NEVER DIES DOLL SET
Exclusive Premiere (1998) *Left*

These nicely boxed dolls are terrific future collectibles. They came in several costume variations.

"James Bond" (in naval uniform)   *Mint $10*
"Wai Lin"   *Mint $10*
"Elliot Carver"   *Mint $10*

291. DR. NO DOLL SET
Exclusive Premiere (1998) *Opposite page*

This second set of dolls released by Exclusive Premiere are from characters featured in the first Bond movie, DR. NO.

"James Bond"   *Mint $10*
"Dr. No"   *Mint $10*
"Honey Rider"   *Mint $10*

292. GOLDFINGER DOLL SET
Exclusive Premiere (1998) *Not illustrated*

These dolls are based on characters from 1964's GOLDFINGER:

"James Bond" (in tuxedo)   *Mint $10*
"Oddjob"   *Mint $10*
"Jill Masterson"   *Mint $10*

293. THE SPY WHO LOVED ME DOLL SET
Exclusive Premiere (1998) *Not illustrated*

Based on characters from the 1977 Bond film.

"James Bond"   *Mint $10*
"Anna Amasava"   *Mint $10*
"Jaws"   *Mint $10*

294. BOND WOMEN DOLL SET #1
Exclusive Premiere (1998) *Not illustrated*

Available only through comic book stores, these dolls are nine inches tall and feature likenesses of several favorite Bond women.

"Tracy DiVencenzo"   *Mint $20*
"Jill Masterson"   *Mint $20*
"Pussy Galore"   *Mint $20*

295. BOND WOMEN DOLL SET #2
Exclusive Premiere (1999) *Not illustrated*

Also available only through comic book stores, these dolls are nine inches tall.

"Xenia Onatopp"   *Mint $20*
"Solataire"   *Mint $20*
"Honey Rider"   *Mint $20*

Note: As of this writing there was a possibility these dolls would not be released.

In 1997 and 1998, the following line of 007 collectibles were sold via mail-order by MGM/United Artists:

296. 007 CARD HOLDER
MGM/UA (1997) *Not illustrated*

This aluminum business card holder is embossed with the 007 logo.

New $16

297. 007 I.D. KEY TAG/PEN
MGM/UA (1997) *Not illustrated*

A dual purpose key tag features a "silver bullet' shaped pen. The I.D. tag is molded on both sides with the 007 logo.

New $8

298. STERLING SILVER 007 KEY TAG
MGM/UA (1997) *Not illustrated*

The 007 logo is etched into the key tag.

New $12

299. TOMORROW NEVER DIES MARTINI GLASSES
MGM/UA (1997) *Not illustrated*

The 007 logo and the logo from TOMORROW NEVER DIES are both etched onto this pair of glasses.

New $12

300. MINI ALUMINUM ATTACHE CASE
MGM/UA (1997) *Not illustrated*

A built-in soilar calculator is hidden inside this little case, with a three-color TOMORROW NEVER DIES logo on top.

New $40

301. TOMORROW NEVER DIES MARTINI GLASS
MGM/UA (1997) *Not illustrated*

The logo from TOMORROW NEVER DIES is satin etched into this glass.

New $15

302. 007 GOLDENEYE WATCH
 MGM/UA (1995) *Not illustrated*

Shock and water resistant with a quartz movement, this timepiece also has a stainless steel bezel and laser-cut lighted 007 logo. It comes packaged in a commemorative case, also with the 007 logo.

Mint in Box $65

303. BOND SHUTTER WATCH
 MGM/UA (1996) *Not illustrated*

This watch features a "camera shutter" opening that reveals the James Bond silhouette logo. It's black leather band has "007" etched onto it.

Mint in Box $70

304. 007 MANTLE CLOCK
 MGM/UA (1997) *Not illustrated*

A brushed chrome clock with gold rim, this item has an elegant laser-engraved 007 gun logo.

New $60

305. 007 CONE AM/FM RADIO
 MGM/UA (1997) *Not illustrated*

This 2 1/4-inch by 2-inch radio features a "cone" control system.

New $60

306. TOMORROW NEVER DIES DIVERS WATCH
 MGM/UA (1997) *Not illustrated*

A neat sports watch loaded with an alarm, stopwatch, chronograph and the TOMORROW NEVER DIES and 007 logos.

New $65

307. JAMES BOND ZIPPO LIGHTER SET
Zippo (1996) *Left, top*

A handsome set of lighters comes in a neat '007' display and features poster artwork from all the Sean Connery James Bond films. A 007 logo lighter is also included in this set, which is a bit pricey, but certain to go up in value.

New $229

308. GOLDENEYE COLLECTORS LIGHTER
Zippo (1996) *Not illustrated*

Commemororating the 1995 return of James Bond to the big screen, this Zippo lighter features the poster art from the film and comes pacxked in an attractive tin.

New $25-$30

309. GOLDENEYE LIGHTER SET
Zippo (1996) *Not illustrated*

A companion set of lighters to Zippo's James Bond set (pictured above) these six lighters also come in a great display box with brass and chrome variations on the 007 logo.

New $229

310. TIMOTHY DALTON MODEL KIT
Dimensional Designs (1990) *Left*

A striking likeness of Timothy Dalton, 007 #4, this resin kit is quite a valuable asset to any James Bond collection.

Mint in Box $150

311. YOU ONLY LIVE TWICE
    JAMES BOND AUTOGYRO RE-ISSUE
       Airfix (1997) *Above*

This newly-boxed version of Airfix's classic "Little Nellie" gyro-copter was made available on a limited basis.

New $12

312. TOMORROW NEVER DIES BMW
       Mini-Champs (1998) *Not illustrated*

A follow-up to the GOLDENEYE BMW released in 1995, this edition is based on the gadget-loaded Beemer from the latest James Bond adventure. Another nice window-boxed die-cast.

New $40

313. GOLDENEYE JAMES BOND FIGURE
       Dragon (1996) *Opposite page; bottom right*

An eight-inch vinyl figure, a tuxedo-clad replica of Pierce Brosnant holding the trademark Walther PPK. This model comes in a nice window display box. For the creative collector, the model is also avail-ablke in kit form. The price is the same for either, but the kit model has a more attractive box.

New $40

314. DR. NO MODEL
       Imai (1996) *Right*

While the model itself is not really a good resemblance of either Sean Connery or Ursula Andress, this is a rare and increasingly valuable col-lectible. It's extremely attractive box might help the cost easier to take.

315.   007 SELECTAVISION DISCS
RCA (1980-1985) *Left; top and bottom*

These forerunners to the laser disc, while being virtually useless for viewing today (try finding a player!) boast unique and creative packaging. Most of the movie discs were singles although a few were double discs. As usual, the Connery Bond films are more desirable.

Mint $20-$30

316. GOLDFINGER DELUXE LASER DISC BOXED SET
MGM/UA (1995) *Above*

What a comparison to the Eighties-era first attempts at 007 state-of-the-art viewing on the opposite page! Undoubtably the ultimate edition of GOLDFINGER. This six-disc set not only features the best-yet, THX-ed version of the film itself, it also has dual audio tracks featuring comments by such Bond alumni as directors Guy Hamilton, Peter Hunt and Richard Maibaum.

The real treasures of the discs are the original radio and TV spots, trailers, black-and-white stills and tons more. Expected to rise in value with the advent of DVD discs.

New $100

317. THUNDERBALL DELUXE LASER DISC BOXED SET
MGM/UA (1996) *Not illustrated*

Another fantastic digital transfer, this version of "the biggest Bond of all" has a restored stereo soundtrack. Also included is the rarely seen TV special, THE INCREDIBLE WORLD OF JAMES BOND.

Dual audio tracks feature commentary by director Terence Young, Richard Maibaum, Lois Maxwell and composer John Barry. Other extras include original and re-issue trailers and TV spots, posters, stills and much more. Will surely rise in value.

New $125

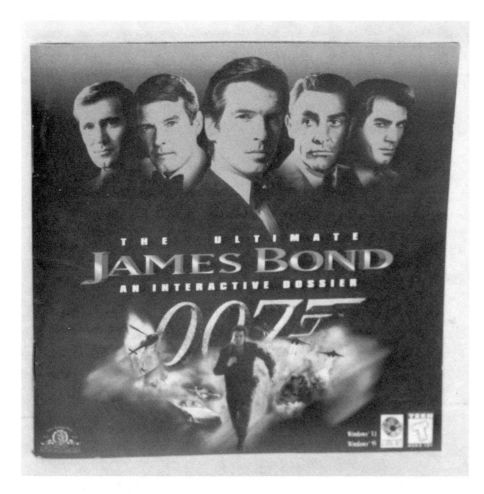

318. THE ULTIMATE JAMES BOND INTERACTIVE DOSSIER
MGM Interactive (1996) *Left*

This fantastic two-CD-ROM set has a massive amount of material dealing with the 007 missions, "declassified" information on the first 17 Bond films, data on the women, the allies, the villians and much more. Hours of fun and diversion are packed into this great software, which comes with a bonus copy of GOLDENEYE on VHS! Currently a real bargain.

New $35

319. JAMES BOND WRISTWATCHES
Fossil (1997) *Not illustrated*

Two versions, a silver edition and gold deluxe edition of this watch were produced, packaged in a tin box featuring the Timothy Dalton silhouette from THE LIVING DAYLIGHTS.

Silver Edition, New $95
Gold Edition, New $140

320. GOLDENEYE PINBALL MACHINE
Gottlieb (1995) *Not illustrated*

For a hefty price you too can relive the first Pierce Brosnan adventure... while trying to pick up enough points for a free replay! Arguably, the ultimate GOLDENEYE collectible.

Mint $4,500

321. ON HER MAJESTY'S SECRET SERVICE GIFT SET
Corgi (1969) *Not illustrated*

This second O.H.M.S.S. gift set (Corgi Catalog No. D978) is just as rare as the #3004 set. Made up of four vehicles, included are the S.P.E.C.T.R.E. Mercedes, Ford Escort, Ford Capri and Tracy's Mercury Cougar.

Mint in Package $300-$350

322. 007 DESKTOP HELICOPTER
Maufacturer unknown (1997) *Not illustrated*

Press a button and you can watch the miniature helicopter from GOLDENEYE zoom around the room. Of course, don't forget that two AA Batterics are required for accurate operation!

Mint $35

Television Spy Toys

Always ready to capitalize on hot movie trends, the television industry made no exception to the spy craze of the early Sixties. Spies had been seen intermittantly on the airwaves during the 1950's in such programs as COUNTERSPY, DANGEROUS ASSIGNMENT and THE HUNTER which, coincidentally, starred Barry Nelson, the first actor to portray James Bond (in the CBS live broadcast of CASINO ROYALE on October 21, 1954.)

Once the James Bond films started to gain in popularity, television producer Norman Felton approached 007's creator Ian Fleming for ideas regarding a secret agent TV series. The basic premise of a world spy organization with an agent named Solo (named after a character from his novel "Goldfinger") were Fleming's contributions.

As Felton developed the show, Bond producers Albert "Cubby" Broccoli and Harry Saltzman threatened legal action for what they saw as an infringement on their spy property, movie rights to most of the James Bond novels. Ian Fleming promptly withdrew, Felton made several changes and THE MAN FROM U.N.C.L.E. was the result.

A slow ratings producer at first U.N.C.L.E. caught on after Christmas 1964 primarily due to a time slot change, personal appearances by the shows' stars and a big network promotional blitz.

By the Fall of 1965 spies of all sorts were thwarting super crime organizations around the TV dial. I-SPY, GET SMART!, THE WILD, WILD WEST, AMOS BURKE - SECRET AGENT (a re-tooled version of BURKE'S LAW) and HONEY WEST (TV's lone female spy) were launched on an eagerly awaiting audience.

Additionally, several British spy series were imported including THE AVENGERS and SECRET AGENT, re-named from DANGERMAN, and given a Johnny Rivers theme song to increase the show's appeal to younger viewers.

Fall 1966 brought a few more spy-based entries, such as MISSION: IMPOSSI-BLE and the ill-conceived GIRL FROM U.N.C.L.E.

Another industry always looking for hot trends has been the toy business and thanks to such companies as A.C. Gilbert, Corgi, Ideal, Mattel, Aladdin and others, no young spy-wannabe had to go without play guns, games, comics and more... inspired by their favorite spy show.

Undoubtably, THE MAN FROM U.N.C.L.E. was the king of licensing, rivaling even James Bond in the number of toys produced. Nearly every series that got on the air had some kind of toy available... from card games to Halloween costumes.

By 1969 most of the spy shows were gone, canceled due to bad creative decisions (such as incorporating a "camp" format in THE MAN FROM U.N.C.L.E.'s third season), declining ratings or Congressional pressure over violence (as was the case with THE WILD, WILD WEST.)

Fortunately, re-runs and home video can let us enjoy these wonderful programs again. But it is the massive legacy of the toys and collectibles that make those childhood memories extra special. As a kid, I remember buying a MAN FROM U.N.C.L.E. coloring book in our local supermarket, WILD, WILD WEST comics at my neighborhood drug store and AVENGERS paperbacks at the tobacco store down the street (he carried all the latest spy books!)

Collecting, reading and displaying these neat items today always sparks an old memory of childhood. And that's the best part for me.

Various spy shows have been broadcast since the big spy boom. However, none were able to re-capture the magic of the Sixties classics. But, when one thinks about it, isn't that what makes all those old shows... and the collectibles they inspired... so special?

The Man From U.N.C.L.E.

(1964-1968)   NBC Network

The greatest toy-producing television series of all, this adventure program starred Robert Vaughn and David McCallum.

After struggling through its debut season and fueled by the James Bond spy mania, audiences began to discover the show. Its ratings caught fire and the merchandising and toy bonanza began.

A disasterous change to a "camp" format in the series' third season brought the show to a premature end half-way through the fourth season.

Many MAN FROM U.N.C.L.E. items are the most valuable collectibles on the toy market today. A sampling are listed in this book.

323. NAPOLEON SOLO MODEL KIT
Aurora (1966) *Far left and below*

An all-plastic assembly kit of Solo scaling a wall, which interlocks with the Illya Kuryakin model (see below) to make a nice diorama.

VG to Mint in Box $175-$200

324. ILLYA KURYAKIN MODEL KIT
Aurora (1966) *Inside left and below*

A bit rarer than the Solo kit above.

VG to Mint in Box $200-$225

325. MAN FROM U.N.C.L.E. LUNCHBOX SET
King-Seely (1966) *Not illustrated*

This steel "dinnerbox" has great artwork by Jack Davis of TV GUIDE fame.

VG to Mint $200-$225

326. MAN FROM U.N.C.L.E. CAR KIT
     AMT (1967) *Above*

Equipped with flame throwers and rocket launchers, of course.

VG to Mint in Box $175-$200

327. MAN FROM U.N.C.L.E. BOARD GAME
     Ideal (1967) *See Catalog Pages*

A bright and colorful box top featuring Robert Vaughn A fairly common item.

VG to Mint $30-$40

328. THRUSH RAY-GUN AFFAIR GAME
     Milton-Bradley (1966) *Right, center*

The rarest of the U.N.C.L.E. board games, this oversized edition has the titular plastic ray-gun, game board, four hide-outs, four agents, four vehicles and four decoder cards.

VG to Mint $100-$125

329. SHOOT OUT! BOARD GAME
     Milton-Bradley (1965) *Right, bottom*

A plastic marble gamethat has two players trying to be the first to spell U.N.C.L.E. Guess it was too corny to call this game "Cry U.N.C.L.E.!

VG to Mint $80-$100

330. MAN FROM U.N.C.L.E. CARD GAME
Milton-Bradley (1965) *Not illustrated*

Quite a common item, but still a good collectible.

VG to Mint $20-$25

331. ILLYA KURYAKIN CARD GAME
Milton-Bradley (1966) *Below*

Very similar to the above game, but this one featured heart-throb David McCallum.

VG to Mint $20-$25

332. MAN FROM U.N.C.L.E. PAPERBACK BOOK SERIES
Ace Books (1965-1968) *Not illustrated*

This set of 23 original novels all have nice color photo covers and some, such as "The Vampire Affair", making pretty good reading. Note that the last five releases are worth considerably more due to low distribution numbers as the TV series wound down.

1.	The Thousand Coffins Affair	*VG to Mint*	*$2-$4*
2.	The Doomsday Affair	*VG to Mint*	*$2-$4*
3.	The Copenhagen Affair	*VG to Mint*	*$2-$4*
4.	The Dagger Affair	*VG to Mint*	*$2-$4*
5.	The Mad Scientist Affair	*VG to Mint*	*$2-$4*
6.	The Vampire Affair	*VG to Mint*	*$3-$5*
7.	The Radioactive Camel Affair	*VG to Mint*	*$3-$5*
8.	The Monster Wheel Affair	*VG to Mint*	*$3-$6*
9.	The Diving Dames Affair	*VG to Mint*	*$4-$8*
10.	The Assasination Affair	*VG to Mint*	*$4-$8*
11.	The Invisibility Affair	*VG to Mint*	*$4-$8*
12.	The Mind-Twisters Affair	*VG to Mint*	*$5-$10*
13.	The Rainbow Affair	*VG to Mint*	*$5-$10*
14.	The Cross of Gold Affair	*VG to Mint*	*$5-$10*
15.	The Utopia Affair	*VG to Mint*	*$5-$10*
16.	The Splintered Sunglasses Affair	*VG to Mint*	*$5-$10*
17.	The Hollow Crown Affair	*VG to Mint*	*$8-$18*
18.	The Unfair Fare Affair	*VG to Mint*	*$8-$18*
19.	The Power Cube Affair	*VG to Mint*	*$10-$20*
20.	The Corfu Affair	*VG to Mint*	*$10-$25*
21.	The Thinking Machine Affair	*VG to Mint*	*$15-$30*
22.	The Ston-Cold-Dead in the Market Affair	*VG to Mint*	*$15-$30*
23.	The Finger in the Sky Affair	*VG to Mint*	*$20-$35*

333. ILLYA KURYAKIN GUN SET
Ideal (1966) *Right*

A clip-firing plastic pistol with U.N.C.L.E. badge and I.D. card make up this set.

VG to Mint in Box $250-$300

334. NAPOLEON SOLO GUN SET
Ideal (1965) *See Catalog Pages*

An attractively packaged set that includes a rifle conversion pistol, U.N.C.L.E. badge and I.D. card.

VG to Mint in Box $450-$500

335. MAN FROM U.N.C.L.E. SECRET SERVICE GUN
Ideal (1965) *See Catalog Pages*

Pistol, holster, U.N.C.L.E. badge and I.D. card make up this set featuring a picture of Robert Vaughn.

VG to Mint in Box $200-$250

336. MAN FROM U.N.C.L.E. THRUSH RIFLE
Ideal (1966) *Not illustrated*

An extremely rare item, this 3-foot long cap-firing rifle is valued highly among collectors.

VG to Mint in Box $775-$825

337. ILLYA KURYAKIN "SPECIAL" LIGHTER GUN
Ideal (1966) *Not illustrated*

A cap-firing cigarette lighter (with fake cigarettes), this neat item also has a secret radio compartment.

VG to Mint $130-$150

338. MAN FROM U.N.C.L.E.
   SECRET WEAPON SET
Ideal (1965) *Right*

A cap gun with clip-loading magazine, silver I.D. card, U.N.C.L.E. badge, wallet, holster, two grenades and grenade holster comprise this great set.

VG to Mint in Box $240-$275

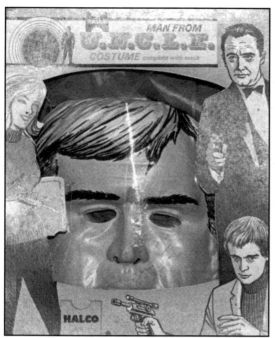

339. MAN FROM U.N.C.L.E. HALLOWEEN COSTUME
Halco (1965-1967) *Left*

Available in two versions, neither looked much like the show's stars.

Napoleon Solo	*VG to Mint in Box*	*$125-$150*
Illya Kuryakin	*VG to Mint in Box*	*$125-$150*

340. U.N.C.L.E. COUNTERSPY OUTFIT
Marx (1966) *Not illustrated*

An extremely colorful box was jam-packed with these super-spy accessories: trench coat, pistol, shoulder holster, scope, silencer, gun extension, launcher barrel plus many more gadgets and disguises.

VG to Mint in Box $175-$200

341. MAN FROM U.N.C.L.E. GUM CARDS
Topps (1965) *Not illustrated*

A 55-card set of black and white photos from the TV series which, when pieced together, form a giant photo on the back.

Complete Set	*Mint*	*$75*
Wrapper	*Mint*	*$30-$40*
Wax Box	*Mint*	*$75-$100*

342. MAN FROM U.N.C.L.E. MYSTERY PUZZLES
Milton-Bradley (1965) *Below*

There were four different puzzles released. Each included a storybook and not-so-hard mystery to solve.

1.	The Microfilm Affair	*Mint in Box*	*$40-$50*
2.	The Vital Observation	*Mint in Box*	*$40-$50*
3.	The Impossible Escape	*Mint in Box*	*$40-$50*
4.	The Loyal Groom	*Mint in Box*	*$40-$50*

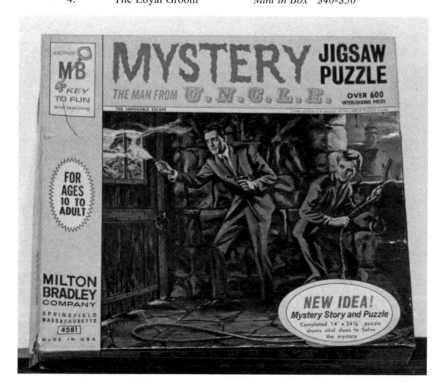

343. MAN FROM U.N.C.L.E. TARGET GAME
Ideal (1965) *Not illustrated*

A cardboard target game with a building front populated by THRUSH agents, who can be shot with a plastic dart gun.

VG to Mint in Box $75-$100

344. MAN FROM U.N.C.L.E. VIEWMASTER SET
Sawyers/GAF (1965) *Not illustrated*

"The Very Important Zombie Affair" in 3-D comes with a story booklet.

VG to Mint in Package $40-$50

345. MAN FROM U.N.C.L.E.
   THRUSH BUSTER CAR
   Corgi (1966) *Top, center, bottom*

A die-cast blue metal Olsmobile with figures of Solo and Kuryakin included. Also came with a "Waverly Flicker Ring". Note extremely rare white version of car in top photo, and cover of box in bottom photo.

VG to Mint in Box $150-$175

346. MAN FROM U.N.C.L.E.
   "HUSKY" THRUSHBUSTER CAR
   Corgi (1966) *Not illustrated*

A smaller version of the Thrushbuster, it was released on two different blister-pack cards.

VG to Mint in Package $75-$100

THE MAN FROM
U.N.C.L.E.
FAMOUS TV SPIES
ACTION FIGURES

16120 NAPOLEON SOLO ACTION FIGURE. Superbly-modeled likeness of the man U.N.C.L.E. sends in when things get rough, Solo is over 11" tall and you can make him fire a cap in his pistol when you release his arm. He comes with white shirt, black pants and shoes— and you may add a whole world of other outfits and accessories.

16125 ILLYA KURYAKIN ACTION FIGURE. Solo's flaxen-haired associate agent is nearly 12" high, and holds a working pistol that fires a cap when you release his arm (caps not included). Illya wears black sweater, pants and shoes. Get him all the other outfits and equipment he needs in the 7 sets shown below.

Accessories and Apparel for every U.N.C.L.E. Agent

16271 TARGET SET. Includes: "Bulletproof" vest; 3 targets with stands; Action Bazooka that fires 3 harmless shells (included); and working binoculars.

16272 JUMP SUIT SET. Includes: Complete jump suit with boots and helmet with chin strap; 28" diam. working parachute and pack; cap-firing Tommy gun with scope.

16273 ARMAMENT SET. Includes: All-weather jacket, military beret, cap-firing pistol with 4 special attachments: Barrel extension, bipod stand, rifle butt and telescopic sight; knife; working binoculars; accessory belt with utility pouch and 4 grenades.

U.N.C.L.E. Membership Card and Identification Badge included with each Solo and Illya figure.

16274 SCUBA SET. Provides complete, authentically-designed equipment to prepare U.N.C.L.E. agents for underwater espionage. Includes: Scuba jacket, swim trunks, air tanks, tank bracket, tubes and knife.

16275 ARSENAL SET No. 1. Includes spring-action bazooka with 3 shells, cap-firing high-powered rifle, cap-firing demountable gun with attachments for converting to rifle.

16276 ARSENAL SET No. 2. Includes: Cap-firing rifle with telescopic sight, grenade belt and 4 grenades. Like all these accessory sets, this equipment may also be used with James Bond or Moon McDare.

16277 PISTOL CONVERSION KIT. Includes: all parts to make cap-firing pistol into U.N.C.L.E. rifle, including bipod, rifle butt, barrel extension and telescopic sight. Also working binoculars.

347. NAPOLEON SOLO ACTION FIGURE
Gilbert (1965) *Opposite page*

A 12-inch likeness of Robert Vaughn, with a spring-loaded arm that fires a cap pistol. Shirt, shoes, I.D. card, U.N.C.L.E. badge and instruction sheet are included.

Mint in Box $100-$120

348. ILLYA KURYAKIN ACTION FIGURE
Gilbert (1965) *Opposite page*

This figure has black pants and sweater, shoes and the same accessories as the Solo doll above.

Mint in Box $100-$120

349. U.N.C.L.E. TARGET SET
Gilbert (1965) *Opposite page*

Bullet-proof vest, three targets, a bazooka, binoculars and three shells.

Mint in Package $40-$50

350. ARMAMENT SET
Gilbert (1965) *Opposite page*

Jacket, beret, cap-firing pistol with attachments, grenade belt, accessory pouch and binoculars.

Mint in Package $30-$40

351. U.N.C.L.E. SCUBA SET
Gilbert (1965) *Opposite page*

Swim trunks, scuba jacket, air tanks and knife.

Mint in Package $45-$60

352. U.N.C.L.E. JUMP SUIT SET
Gilbert (1965) *Opposite page*

A jump suit with boots, chin-strapped helmet, parachute and pack plus a cap-firing machine gun.

Mint in Package $45-$60

353. U.N.C.L.E. ARSENAL SET #1
Gilbert (1965) *Opposite page*

Machine gun, bazooka, three shells, cap-firing pistol with attachments.

Mint in Package $25-$30

354. U.N.C.L.E. ARSENAL SET #2
Gilbert (1965) *Opposite page*

A mini-set of grenade belt and THRUSH rifle.

Mint in Package $15-$20

355. U.N.C.L.E. PISTOL CONVERSION SET
Gilbert (1965) *Opposite page*

Another mini-set of binoculars and a pistol with attachments.

Mint in Package $15-$20

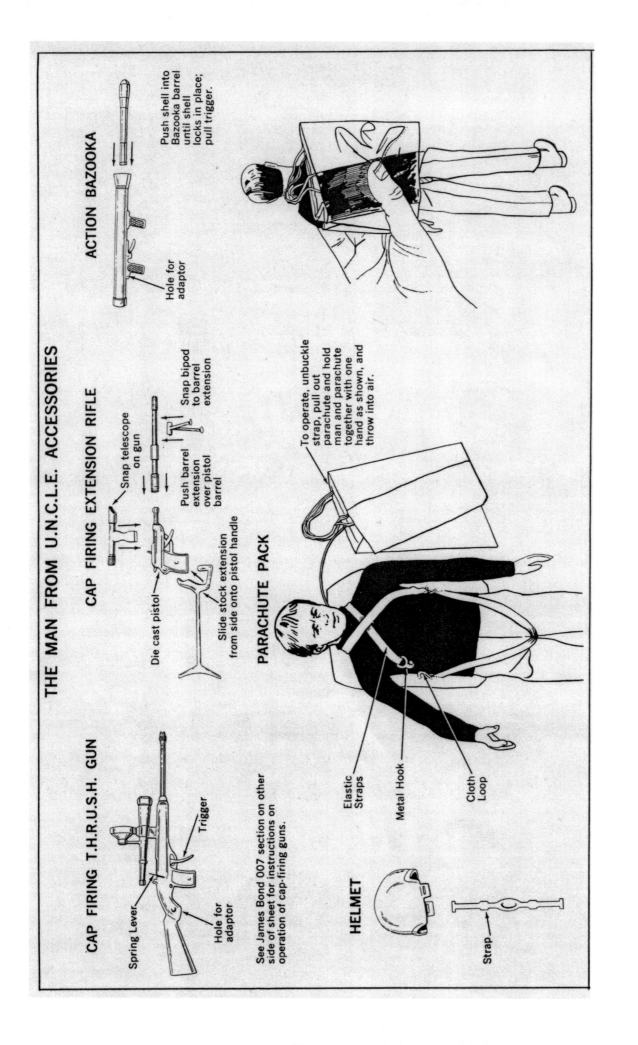

THE MAN FROM U.N.C.L.E. ACCESSORIES

CAP FIRING T.H.R.U.S.H. GUN

Spring Lever

Trigger

Hole for adaptor

See James Bond 007 section on other side of sheet for instructions on operation of cap-firing guns.

CAP FIRING EXTENSION RIFLE

Snap telescope on gun

Die cast pistol

Slide stock extension from side onto pistol handle

Push barrel extension over pistol barrel

Snap bipod to barrel extension

ACTION BAZOOKA

Hole for adaptor

Push shell into Bazooka barrel until shell locks in place; pull trigger.

PARACHUTE PACK

Elastic Straps

Metal Hook

Cloth Loop

To operate, unbuckle strap, pull out parachute and hold man and parachute together with one hand as shown, and throw into air.

HELMET

Strap

**356. MAN FROM U.N.C.L.E.
SPY TRICKS**
Gilbert (1965) *Right*

Seven U.N.C.L.E.-embellished magic tricks in a nicely illustrated box.

VG to Mint in Box $100-$125

357. ORIGINAL MUSIC FROM THE MAN FROM U.N.C.L.E.   RECORD ALBUM
RCA Victor (1965) *Not illustrated*

A great album cover, but with disapointing arrangements of Jerry Goldsmith's U.N.C.L.E. music by Hugo Montenegro.

VG to Mint $25-$30

358. MORE MUSIC FROM THE MAN FROM U.N.C.L.E.   RECORD ALBUM
RCA Victor (1966) *Not illustrated*

A second Montenegro miscue, but another terrific album cover.

VG to Mint $30-$40

359. MAN FROM U.N.C.L.E.   COMIC BOOK SERIES
Gold Key (1965-1969) *Issue #4 see page 97; others not illustrated*

A 22-issue set. All have nice photo covers and original stories and art.

1.	The Explosive Affair	*Good to Mint*	*$10-$35*
2.	The Fortune Cookie Affair	*Good to Mint*	*$10-$35*
3.	The Deadly Devices Affair	*Good to Mint*	*$10-$35*
4.	The Rip Van Solo Affair	*Good to Mint*	*$10-$35*
5.	The Ten Little Uncles Affair	*Good to Mint*	*$10-$35*
6.	The Three Blind Mice Affair	*Good to Mint*	*$10-$35*
7.	The Pixilated Puzzle Affair	*Good to Mint*	*$10-$35*
8.	The Floating People Affair	*Good to Mint*	*$10-$35*
9.	The Spirit of St. Louis Affair	*Good to Mint*	*$10-$35*
10.	The Trojan Horse Affair	*Good to Mint*	*$10-$35*
11.	The Three-Story Giant Affair	*Good to Mint*	*$10-$35*
12.	The Dead Man's Diary Affair		*Good to Mint $10-$35*
13.	The Flying Clowns Affair	*Good to Mint*	*$10-$35*
14.	The Great Brain Drain Affair	*Good to Mint*	*$10-$35*
15.	The Animal Agents Affair	*Good to Mint*	*$10-$35*
16.	The Instant Disaster Affair	*Good to Mint*	*$10-$35*
17.	The Deadly Visions Affair	*Good to Mint*	*$10-$35*
18.	The Alien Affair	*Good to Mint*	*$10-$35*
19.	The Knight in Shining Armor Affair	*Good to Mint*	*$10-$35*
20.	The Deep-Freeze Affair	*Good to Mint*	*$10-$35*
21.	Reprint of Issue #10	*Good to Mint*	*$10-$35*
22.	Reprint of Issue #7	*Good to Mint*	*$10-$35*

360. MAN FROM U.N.C.L.E. SHOOTING ARCADE
Marx (1966) *Left, top (See also Catalog Pages)*

This game came in a large and small version. The object of both is to shoot THRUSH agents (no kidding!)

Large Version   *VG to Mint in Box $225-$250*
Small Version   *VG to Mint in Box $100-$125*

361. MAN FROM U.N.C.L.E. TARGET GAME
Marx (1966) *See Catalog Pages*

Sold exclusively at Sears, this large cardboard "headquarters" target set included 12 plastic U.N.C.L.E. and THRUSH agents along with two pistols, six darts, two grenades and an instruction sheet.

VG to Mint $300-$350

362. MAN FROM U.N.C.L.E. PINBALL GAME
Marx (1966) *Not illustrated*

"The Pinball Affair" has great graphics and comes with 10 marbles and a single flipper.

VG to Mint $100-$125

363. SECRET CODE WHEEL PINBALL GAME
Marx (1966) *Not illustrated*

Much more elaborate and rarer than the above game, 12 small prizes are won when the player locates the right door with the pinball marble.

VG to Mint $275-$300

364. MAN FROM U.N.C.L.E. MAGIC SLATE
Watkins-Strathmore (1965) *Left, center*

An extremely scarce collectible, these two items have punch-out figures of either Solo or Kuryakin. Orginally priced at just 29-cents each.

Mint $125-$140

365. MAN FROM U.N.C.L.E. CREDENTIALS
Ideal (1965) *Left, bottom*

An I.D. wallet, passport, U.N.C.L.E., badge and silver I.D. card are part of this collectible.

Good to Mint $60-$75

366. ILLYA KURYAKIN JUNIOR PUZZLES
     Milton-Bradley (1966) *Above, left and right*

A 100-piece puzzle. Two different versions were produced.

ILLYA'S BATTLE BELOW   *Good to Mint $60-$75*
ILLYSA CRUSHES THRUSH   *Good to Mint $60-$75*

367. MAN FROM U.N.C.L.E. FINGER PRINT KIT
     Manufacturer unknown (1966) *Right, center*

A very rare item, this finger print kit actually works! Nice graphics.

VG to Mint $100-$125

368. MAN FROM U.N.C.L.E. FOTO FANTASTIKS
     Eberhard-Faber (1965) *Right, bottom*

Four differents sets of these stickers were produced, each consisting of
six photos that could be colored with pencil and brush.

VG to Mint $50-$60

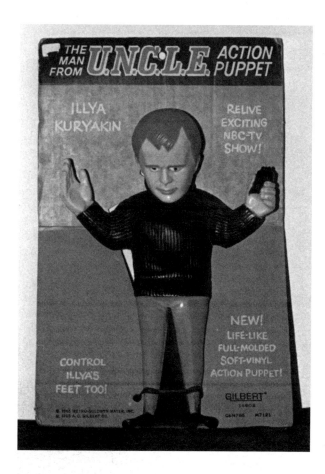

369. MAN FROM U.N.C.L.E. ACTION PUPPET
Gilbert (1965) *Left, top*

Illya is the slightly distorted subject of this item, which is a 13-inch like-ness of David McCallum.

Mint on Card $150

370. MAN FROM U.N.C.L.E. PISTOL CANE
Marx (1966) *Bottom, left*

A well-illustrated card displays the cap and bullet-shooting cane, which comes with eight bullets and one shell.)

Mint on Card $150-$175

371. MAN FROM U.N.C.L.E. FINGER PUPPETS
Dean (1966) *Bottom, right*

This extremely rare U.N.C.L.E. piece contains six separate puppets dis-played in a theater-type box adorned with U.N.C.L.E. artwork. A ticket to this show is increasingly costly.

Mint in Box $300

372. MAN FROM U.N.C.L.E. ATTACHE CASE
Ideal (1965) *Opposite page, top and inset*

The U.N.C.L.E. answer to James Bond's best-selling attache case. This wonderful and rare collectible features an assortment of gadgetry. A passport, I.D. card, wallet, U.N.C.L.E. badge, cap grenade, pistol with ammo clip and a secret message sender are among the contents.

Good to Mint $250-$300

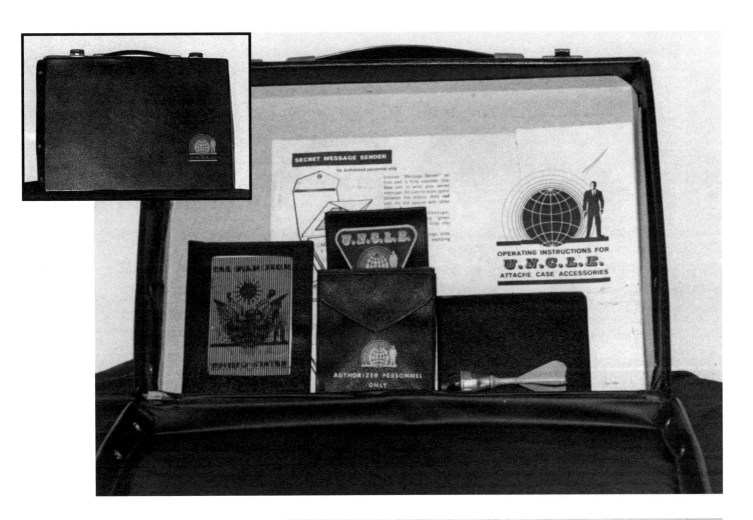

373. MAN FROM U.N.C.L.E. WALLET

Ideal (1966) *Right, center*

The U.N.C.L.E. logo graces the front of the wallet, while Agents Solo and Kuryakin adorn the back.

Good to Mint $60-$75

374. MAN FROM U.N.C.L.E. PLAYING CARDS

Ed-U-Cards (1965) *Right, bottom*

This 54-card set has an assortment of 40 action photos of Napoleon and Illya. Having the display card adds greatly to the value.

Complete Set   *Mint $25*
Complete Set with Display Card   *Mint $50*

375. MAN FROM U.N.C.L.E. MAGAZINE
    Leo Margulies (1966-1968) *Not illustrated*

These paper-bound magazines originally cost 50-cents and had black and white photos of the men from U.N.C.L.E. on both front and back covers.

VOLUME ONE

#1	The Howling Teenagers Affair	*Good to Mint*	*$10-15*
#2	The Beauty and the Beast Affair	*Good to Mint*	*$10-15*
#3	The Unspeakable Affair	*Good to Mint*	*$10-15*
#4	The World's End Affair	*Good to Mint*	*$10-15*
#5	The Vanishing Act Affair	*Good to Mint*	*$10-15*
#6	The Ghost Rider's Affair	*Good to Mint*	*$10-15*

VOLUME TWO

#1	The Cat and Mouse Affair	*Good to Mint*	*$10-15*
#2	The Brainwash Affair	*Good to Mint*	*$10-15*
#3	The Moby Dick Affair	*Good to Mint*	*$10-15*
#4	The Thrush from Thrush Affair	*Good to Mint*	*$10-15*
#5	The Goliath Affair	*Good to Mint*	*$10-15*
#6	The Light Kill Affair	*Good to Mint*	*$10-15*

VOLUME THREE

#1	The Deadly Dark Affair	*Good to Mint*	*$10-15*
#2	The Hungry World Affair	*Good to Mint*	*$10-15*
#3	The Dolls of Death Affair	*Good to Mint*	*$10-15*
#4	The Synthetic Storm Affair	*Good to Mint*	*$10-15*
#5	The Ugly Man Affair	*Good to Mint*	*$10-15*
#6	The Electronic Frankenstein Affair	*Good to Mint*	*$10-15*

VOLUME FOUR

#1	The Genghis Khan Affair	*Good to Mint*	*$10-15*
#2	The Man From Yesterday Affair	*Good to Mint*	*$10-15*
#3	The Mind Sweeper Affair	*Good to Mint*	*$10-15*
#4	The Volcano Box Affair	*Good to Mint*	*$12-18*
#5	The Pillars of Salt Affair	*Good to Mint*	*$12-18*
#6	The Million Monster Affair (***)	*Good to Mint*	*$25-50*

(***)   This is the rarest of the U.N.C.L.E. magazines.

The Girl From U.N.C.L.E.   1966-1967   NBC Network

This series was a spin-off of THE MAN FROM U.N.C.L.E. The show, starring Stephanie Powers, lasted only one season primarily as a result of bad scripts and subsequently poor ratings. However, a few highly collectible toy items were produced and some of these have become the most sought-after spy toy collectibles on the market today.

376. GIRL FROM U.N.C.L.E. DOLL
    Mary (1967) *Not illustrated*

The rarest 'Girl' collectible, this 11-inch doll came with 30 different accessories and a nicely illustrated box featuring Stephanie Powers. Maybe you've got one in the attic!

Good to Mint in Box $500-$750

377. GIRL FROM U.N.C.L.E. RECORD ALBUM
    MGM Records (1966) *Not illustrated*

A great photo of Ms. Powers is on the cover of this open-up vinyl disc. To be considered Mint condition the album must not be "punched."

VG to Mint $25-$40

THE MAN FROM U.N.C.L.E. NAPOLEON SOLO GUN

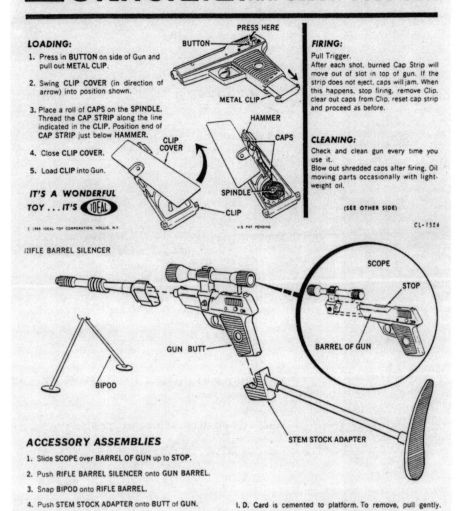

LOADING:

1. Press in BUTTON on side of Gun and pull out METAL CLIP.

2. Swing CLIP COVER (in direction of arrow) into position shown.

3. Place a roll of CAPS on the SPINDLE. Thread the CAP STRIP along the line indicated in the CLIP. Position end of CAP STRIP just below HAMMER.

4. Close CLIP COVER.

5. Load CLIP into Gun.

IT'S A WONDERFUL TOY . . . IT'S IDEAL

© 1965 IDEAL TOY CORPORATION, HOLLIS, N.Y.

U.S. PAT. PENDING

FIRING:

Pull Trigger.
After each shot, burned Cap Strip will move out of slot in top of gun. If the strip does not eject, caps will jam. When this happens, stop firing, remove Clip, clear out caps from Clip, reset cap strip and proceed as before.

CLEANING:

Check and clean gun every time you use it.
Blow out shredded caps after firing. Oil moving parts occasionally with light-weight oil.

(SEE OTHER SIDE)

CL-1526

ACCESSORY ASSEMBLIES

1. Slide SCOPE over BARREL OF GUN up to STOP.

2. Push RIFLE BARREL SILENCER onto GUN BARREL.

3. Snap BIPOD onto RIFLE BARREL.

4. Push STEM STOCK ADAPTER onto BUTT of GUN.

I. D. Card is cemented to platform. To remove, pull gently.

ILLYA "K" SPECIAL

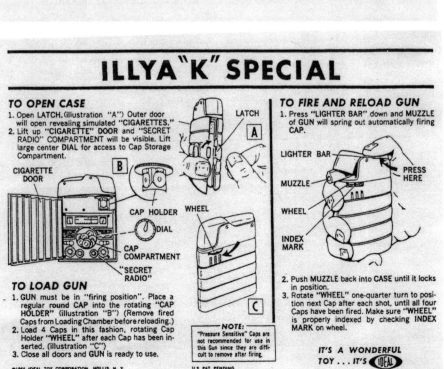

TO OPEN CASE

1. Open LATCH. (Illustration "A") Outer door will open revealing simulated "CIGARETTES."

2. Lift up "CIGARETTE" DOOR and "SECRET RADIO" COMPARTMENT will be visible. Lift large center DIAL for access to Cap Storage Compartment.

TO LOAD GUN

1. GUN must be in "firing position". Place a regular round CAP into the rotating "CAP HOLDER" (Illustration "B") (Remove fired Caps from Loading Chamber before reloading.)

2. Load 4 Caps in this fashion, rotating Cap Holder "WHEEL" after each Cap has been inserted. (Illustration "C")

3. Close all doors and GUN is ready to use.

© 1966 IDEAL TOY CORPORATION, HOLLIS, N.Y.

NOTE:
"Pressure Sensitive" Caps are not recommended for use in this Gun since they are difficult to remove after firing.

U.S. PAT. PENDING

TO FIRE AND RELOAD GUN

1. Press "LIGHTER BAR" down and MUZZLE of GUN will spring out automatically firing CAP.

2. Push MUZZLE back into CASE until it locks in position.

3. Rotate "WHEEL" one-quarter turn to position next Cap after each shot, until all four Caps have been fired. Make sure "WHEEL" is properly indexed by checking INDEX MARK on wheel.

IT'S A WONDERFUL TOY . . . IT'S IDEAL

378. GIRL FROM U.N.C.L.E. SECRET AGENT WRISTWATCH
Bradley (1966) *Not illustrated*

Another rare item, this watch came in a nice case. The watch's pink face has a picture of Power's character, April Dancer, on it.

VG to Mint $275-$350

379. GIRL FROM U.N.C.L.E. MODEL CAR KIT
AMT (1967) *Not illustrated*

Talk about maximizing sales. This model is the exact same car sold as the man from U.N.C.L.E.'s car... just with different box art! Finding this item is difficult.

VG to Mint $400-$500

380. GIRL FROM U.N.C.L.E. COMIC BOOKS
Gold Key (1966-1967) *Not illustrated*

A five issue set, the first comic is slightly more valuable than the others.

Comic #1	*Good to Mint*	*$25-$30*
Comics #2 - #5	*Good to Mint*	*$15-$20*

381. GIRL FROM U.N.C.L.E. HALLOWEEN COSTUME
Halco (1967) *Not illustrated*

JThe increasing value of this collectible is the only thing scary.

VG to Mint in Box $250-$300

382. GIRL FROM U.N.C.L.E. MAGAZINE
Leo Margulies (1966-1967) *Not illustrated*

This digest-type magazine had an identical format as the companion MAN FROM U.N.C.L.E. Magazine. Due to the series' short run, only a few issues were produced.

VOLUME ONE

#1	The Shiek from Araby Affair	*Good to Mint*	*$10-15*
#2	The Velvet Voice Affair	*Good to Mint*	*$10-15*
#3	The Burning Air Affair	*Good to Mint*	*$10-15*
#4	The Deadly Drug Affair	*Good to Mint*	*$10-15*
#5	The Mesmerizing Affair	*Good to Mint*	*$10-15*
#6	The Stolen Spaceman Affair	*Good to Mint*	*$10-15*

VOLUME TWO

#1	The Sinister Satellite Affair	*Good to Mint*	*$10-15*

383. GIRL FROM U.N.C.L.E. PAPERBACK BOOKS
Ace (1966) *Not illustrated*

Only two books were ever published.

#1	The Birds of a Feather Affair	*Good to Mint*	*$8-$10*
#2	The Blazing Affair	*Good to Mint*	*$8-$10*

The Wild, Wild West

(1965-1969)   CBS Network

This "James Bond in the Old West" series starred Robert Conrad and Ross Martin as Secret Service Agents James West and Artemus Gordon. Still a highly popular program in syndication, it unfortunately, had very few merchandising tie-ins. Given the appealing premise and solid characters, it is surprising more licensing was not done.

384.   WILD, WILD WEST LUNCHBOX AND THERMOS
        Aladdin (1968) *Below, left and right*

A great steel lunchbox with plastic Thermos, beautifully decorated. The artwork depicts West and Gordon in action.

Good to Mint (including Thermos) $150-$175

385.   WILD, WILD WEST BOARD GAME
        Transogram (1966) *Not illustrated*

An extremely rare board game. The box cover features West and the private train, plus an inset photo of Conrad and Martin.

Good to Mint $250-$275

386. WILD, WILD WEST COMIC BOOK SERIES
Gold Key (1966-1969) *Left, top and center*

This seven book set has nice photo covers of the show's stars as well as original stories. Note the back cover's "pin-up."

Issues #1 - #2	*Mint*	*$50*
Issues #2 - #7	*Mint*	*$40*

387. WILD, WILD WEST SECRET SLEEVE GUN
Ray Plastics (1966) *Not illustrated*

The rarest of the WWW collectibles, this neat pistol was on a spring loaded mechanism that popped out from under a shirt sleeve... just like James West's.

Mint $125-$150

388. WILD, WILD WEST JAMES WEST DOLL
Exclusive Premiere (1998) *Not illustrated*

Part of the "Best of the West" series, this doll comes in a nicely designed window package. The likeness of Robert Conrad comes dressed in the famous (and tight!) blue outfit.

Retail Price $20

389. WILD, WILD WEST COLLECTORS EDITION VHS TAPES
Columbia House (1995) *Not illustrated*

Released as part of the "Retro TV" series, 25 volumes of classic digitally mastered WWW episodes were made available on VHS videocassettes. All of the two-show cassettes come in a case featuring black and white stills from the program.

Pilot Episode	*Retail*	*$15*
Other Episodes	*Retail*	*$25*

390. WILD, WILD WEST CARD SET
English-Barrantee (1969) *Not illustrated*

A 75-card set based on the series, these cards were produced in England.

Complete Set	*Mint*	*$75-$100*

391. WILD, WILD WEST PAPERBACK BOOK
Signet (1965) *Left, bottom*

Based on the pilot episode, "The Night of the Double-Edged Knife", this novel features black and white photos of Robert Conrad on front and back covers.

Good to Mint $15-$20

The Avengers

(1966-1969)   ABC Network

Undoubtably the classiest of the Sixties spy shows, The Avengers follows the exploits of suave and debonair British agent John Steed (Patrick McNee) and the resourceful and beautiful Mrs. Emma Peel (Diana Rigg.)

After Diana Rigg's departure from the show, Linda Thorson joined the cast as Tara King. (One can also include Honor Blackman, an earlier Steed partner. However these episodes were not broadcast in the United States in the 1960's.)

Very few toy and merchandise items were made available in the U.S. and those that were are among the rarest and most expensive spy toy collectibles around.

392.   THE AVENGERS PAPERBACK BOOK SERIES
    Berkeley (1967-1969) *Volume #2 above; others not illustrated*

Each of these nine novels has a nice color cover featuring Steed and Mrs. Peel, and sometimes Tara King.

1.	The Laugh Was on Lazarus	*Good to Mint*	*$8-$10*
2.	The Floating Game	*Good to Mint*	*$8-$10*
3.	The Passing of Gloria Mundy	*Good to Mint*	*$10-$12*
4.	Heil Harris	*Good to Mint*	*$10-$12*
5.	The Afrit Affair	*Good to Mint*	*$12-$15*
6.	The Drowned Queen	*Good to Mint*	*$12-$15*
7.	The Gold Bomb	*Good to Mint*	*$12-$15*
8.	The Magnetic Man	*Good to Mint*	*$12-$15*
9.	Moon Express	*Good to Mint*	*$12-$15*

393.   THE AVENGERS CORGI CAR SET
    Corgi (1966) *Not illustrated*

The most valuable of all Corgi die-cast spy vehicles. This set includes Steed's Bentley and Mrs. Peels's Lotus Elantra. The display box is a very attractive collectible by itself.

Mint in Box $500-$550

394.   EMMA PEEL DOLL
    Fairlite (1966) *Not illustrated*

A ten-inch likeness of Diana Rigg complete with three outfits, metal stand and pistol. Attractively boxed.

VG to Mint $850-$1,000

395.   THE AVENGERS COMIC BOOK
    Gold Key (1968) *Not illustrated*

This one-shot comic, which contains two separate stories, has a nice photo cover of Steed and Peel.

Mint $150-$170

396. THE AVENGERS TRADING CARD SETS
Cornerstone (1993-1995) *Left*

Three separate card sets having both black and white and color pictures. Various sub-sets were included.

Complete Set	*VG to Mint*	*$25-$35*
Empty Box	*VG to Mint*	*$5-$10*

397. THE AVENGERS JIGSAW PUZZLES
Thomas, Hope and Sankey (1966) *Not illustrated*

Available exclusively at Woolworth's each of these four puzzles came in a nice looking box featuring Steed and Mrs. Peel.

1.	Scene from "Castle of Death"	*Mint*	*$300*
2.	Scene from "Death at Bargain Prices"	*Mint*	*$300*
3.	Scene from "The Master Minds"	*Mint*	*$300*
4.	Railroad Fight Scene	*Mint*	*$300*

398. THE AVENGERS TV GUIDE
TV Guide (1968) *Not illustrated*

The weekly television magazine had a color cover of Patrick McNee and Diana Rigg. An article on them was inside. This was the only time they ever appeared on a TV GUIDE cover.

VG to Mint $20-$25

399. THE AVENGERS TV SCORE ALBUM
Varese (1982) *Not illustrated*

Includes the very best version of Laurie Johnson's wonderful theme music, but very little other Avengers music.

Mint $10

400. THE AVENGERS STEED BOWLER HAT
Lonestar (1966) *Not illustrated*

A rare British toy product. Rare, but doesn't do much else except sit on your head.

VG to Mint $500-$550

401. THE AVENGERS STEED SWORD STICK
Lonestar (1966) *Not illustrated*

The perfect item to accessorize your Steed Bowler Hat. That's obviously what the toy maker in England felt when they came up with this one.

VG to Mint $500-$550

402. THE AVENGERS SHOOTING GAME
Merit (1966) *Not illustrated*

Another British toy tie-in. The only Avengers board game ever produced.

VG to Mint $300-$350

403. THE NEW AVENGERS MODEL KITS
Revell (1979) *Not illustrated*

The 1970's sequel to the original AVENGERS series also featured John Steed. But he was partnered with two new associates, Gambit and Purdy. Revell produced these scale replicas of both THE NEW AVENGERS vehicles, Gambit's Jaguar XJS and Purdy's Triumph TR7. Both models are of equal value.

Mint in Box $75

I-Spy

(1965-1968)   NBC Network

Tennis pro Kelly Robinson (Robert Culp), who was actually the secret agent, was assisted by Alexander Scott (Bill Cosby) in his struggles with enemy agents everywhere.

Shot on location around the world, this series was more adult-oriented fare than other shows of the era. Therefore, there were few toys and merchandise produced.

404.   I-SPY BOARD GAME
   Ideal (1965) *Not illustrated*

A colorful box lid featuring a photo of Robert Culp and Bill Cosby.

VG to Mint $50-$60

405.   I-SPY CARD GAME
   Ideal (1965) *Not illustrated*

This "mini-board" card game came with illustrated cards and a pegboard.

VG to Mint $40-$60

406.   I-SPY TARGET SET
   Ray-Line (1965) *Not illustrated*

A blister-pack set containg pistol, pellet-bullets and three spy figures along with color photos of Culp and Cosby.

VG to Mint $100-$125

407.   I-SPY GUN AND HOLSTER SET
   Ray-Line (1965) *Not illustrated*

Another color blister-pack toy, this set has a blue/black pistol with small pellet-bullets and a black shoulder holster.

VG to Mint $100-$125

408.   I-SPY PAPERBACK BOOK SERIES
   Popular (1965-1967) *Volume #4 above; others not illustrated*

These six novels all had nice photo covers.

1.	I-Spy	*Good to Mint*	*$10-$12*
2.	Masterstroke	*Good to Mint*	*$10-$12*
3.	Superkill	*Good to Mint*	*$10-$12*
4.	Wipeout	*Good to Mint*	*$10-$12*
5.	Countertrap	*Good to Mint*	*$10-$12*
6.	Doomdate	*Good to Mint*	*$10-$12*

409.   I-SPY COMIC BOOK SERIES
   Gold Key (1966-1968) *Not illustrated*

Each of this six-set series has a photo cover of Bill Cosby and Robert Culp, with original stories and artwork.

Issue #1	*Mint*	*$120*
Issues #2 - #6	*Mint*	*$75*

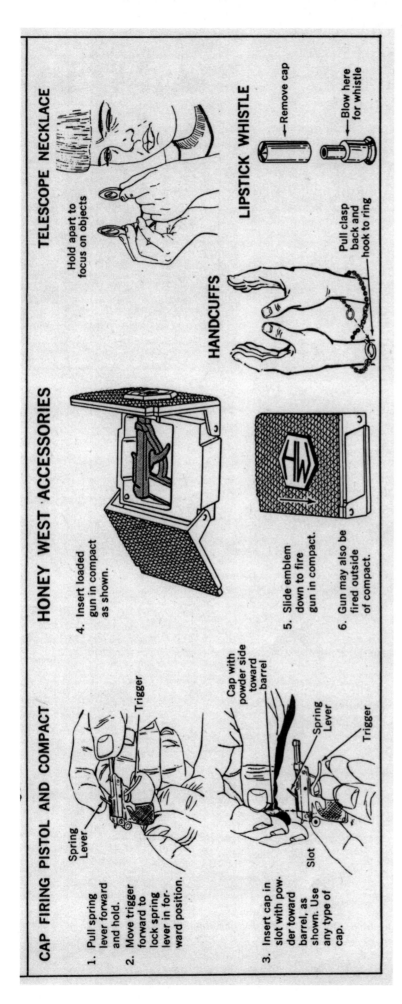

CAP FIRING PISTOL AND COMPACT / HONEY WEST ACCESSORIES / TELESCOPE NECKLACE

TELESCOPE NECKLACE

Hold apart to focus on objects

LIPSTICK WHISTLE

Remove cap

Blow here for whistle

HANDCUFFS

Pull clasp back and hook to ring

HONEY WEST ACCESSORIES

4. Insert loaded gun in compact as shown.

5. Slide emblem down to fire gun in compact.

6. Gun may also be fired outside of compact.

CAP FIRING PISTOL AND COMPACT

Trigger

Spring Lever

1. Pull spring lever forward and hold.

2. Move trigger forward to lock spring lever in forward position.

Cap with powder side toward barrel

Spring Lever

Trigger

3. Insert cap in slot with powder toward barrel, as shown. Use any type of cap.

Slot

Honey West

(1965-1966)   ABC Network

Honey West, the female private eye-spy was portrayed on television by Anne Francis. Unfortunately, the series lasted only one season.

Hip, curvaceous and beautiful, she was made-to-order for the Gilbert doll tie-in. That doll is the primary collectible of the show.

410.   HONEY WEST 11" FIGURE
      Gilbert (1965) *Opposite page*

This doll has moveable arms and legs and comes with Honey's trademark black leotard suit, boots, gold belt with holster and pistol, of course.

VG to Mint in Box $350-$375

411.   HONEY WEST SECRET AGENT OUTFIT
      Gilbert (1965) *Opposite page*

Black trench coat, beret, high-heel shoes, shoulder bag with phone, camera, sunglasses and a compact with a secret compartment containing a pistol.

Mint in Package $85-$100

412.   HONEY WEST KARATE OUTFIT
      Gilbert (1965) *Opposite page*

A karate jacket, belt, headband, pants, sandals and handbook. Also included: a hat box, mirror, brush, comb and a secret lipstick whistle bracelet (that doubles as handcuffs!)

Mint in Package $85-$100

413.   HONEY WEST FORMAL OUTFIT
      Gilbert (1965) *Opposite page*

A full-length evening gown, jacket with ocelot-trimmed collar, cloth bag, hegh heels, secret lipstick whistle and a necklace with a secret telescope.

Mint in Package $85-$100

414. HONEY WEST PET SET
    Gilbert (1965) *Right*

Honey's pet ocelot comes with a leash, clutch bag, high
heel shoes, binoculars, lipstick whistle and hand-cuff
bracelet. A well-dressed ocelot for a lot.

Mint in Package $125-$150

415. HONEY WEST SPY COMPACT SET
    Gilbert (1965) *Right*

This set includes a cap-firing miniature pistol, a compact
with a secret pistol compartment, hat box, telescope/neck-
lace, comb, brush, mirror and high-heel shoes.

Mint in Package $80-$90

416. HONEY WEST EQUIPMENT SET
    Gilbert (1965) *Right*

Also has the cap pistol, working binoculars, high-heel
shoes and glamorous (?) horn-rimmed glasses.

Mint in Package $50-$60

417. HONEY WEST SPY ACCESSORY KIT
    Gilbert (1965) *Right*

Includes telephone handbag, handcuff-bracelet, tele-
scope/necklace and secret lipstick whistle.

Mint in Package $50-$60

418. HONEY WEST COMIC BOOK
    Gold Key (1966) *Not illustrated*

A photo cover of Anne Francis starts off this 32-page
story. A one-shot comic.

Mint $75

HONEY WEST

FAMOUS TV PRIVATE EYE-FULL

16114 HONEY WEST 11" DOLL. You
love her on TV .. and you'll love this
enchanting miniature of glamorous
Anne Francis. She comes with svelte
black leotards and boots. She wears a
gold-color belt and holster, complete
with tiny pistol. She's beautifully-pro-
portioned, with movable arms and
legs. And you can get all sorts of exciting apparel and accessories for
Honey — even her pet ocelot!

HONEY WEST ACCESSORIES

**16261 SECRET
AGENT OUTFIT.**
Black trench coat,
beret and high
heel shoes; shoul-
der bag with
phone; camera
with strap; dark
glasses; compact
with secret com-
partment that
holds miniature
pistol, which fires
cap either from
inside compact or
held in hand.

**16262 KARATE
OUTFIT.** Karate
jacket, belt, head-
band, pants and
sandals. Also hat
box; brush, comb
and mirror; secret
lipstick-whistle;
bracelet that
doubles as hand-
cuffs; even a doll-
size booklet on the
art of Karate!

**16263 FORMAL
OUTFIT.** Glamorous
full-length evening
gown; jacket with
ocelot trimmed
collar; clutch bag;
high heel shoes;
secret lipstick-
whistle; and neck-
lace with secret
telescope.

16264 PET SET. In-
cludes Honey's pet
ocelot complete
with leash, clutch
bag, high heel
shoes, binoculars
that actually work,
lipstick-whistle
and hand-cuff/
bracelet.

**16265 SPY COM-
PACT SET.** Includes
cap-firing minia-
ture pistol, com-
pact with secret
pistol compart-
ment (from which
gun may be fired),
hat box, telescope/
necklace, comb,
brush, mirror and
high-heel shoes.

**16266 EQUIPMENT
SET.** Includes mini-
ature cap firing
pistol, working
binoculars, high
heel shoes, glam-
orous "horn-rim"
glasses.

**16267 SPY ACCES-
SORY SET.** Includes
handbag with at-
tached telephone,
handcuff/bracelet,
telescope/neck-
lace, secret lip-
stick-whistle.

Get Smart!

(1965-1970)   NBC and CBS Networks

Secret Agent 86, Maxwell Smart (played by Don Adams) stumbled his way through an amazing five broadcast seasons on two different networks.

Along with his partner, sexy Agent 99 (Barbara Feldon) they thwarted K.A.O.S. and left some highly collectible toy items along the way. Most of these are very rare.

419.   GET SMART! GUM CARDS
   Don Russ (1966) *Not illustrated*

This 66-card set has black and white photos on the front with quiz riddles on the back.

Complete Set	*VG to Mint*	*$100-$150*
Wrapper	*VG to Mint*	*$25-$40*
Display Box	*VG to Mint*	*$100-$150*

420.   GET SMART! HEADQUARTERS SIGNAL RAY GUN
   Marx (1966) *Not illustrated*

A hand-held pistol comes with a nice drawing of don Adams on the box.

VG to Mint $50-$75

421.   GET SMART! EXPLODING TIME BOMB GAME
   Ideal (1965) *Not illustrated*

Collecting clue cards to make a picture of a KAOS agent while avoiding the ticking time bomb is the object of this game.

Good to Mint $40-$60

422.   GET SMART! MODEL CAR KIT
   AMT (1967) *Not illustrated*

This 1:25 scale model of Agent 86's 1965 Sunbeam sports car is a great collectible.

Good to Mint $75-$100

423.   GET SMART! PEN-RADIO
   MPC (1966) *Not illustrated*

An AM radio shaped like a pen, it comes with an earpiece and clip. Packaged in an attractive window display box.

Good to Mint $45-$75

424.   GET SMART! LUNCH BOX
   King-Seeley (1966) *Not illustrated*

This colorful steel box with Thermos has different artwork on each side.

Mint $200-$225

425. GET SMART! AGENT 99 LIPSTICK RADIO
  MPC (1966) *Right*

A lipstick container version of the GET SMART! Pen Radio.

Good to Mint $45-$75

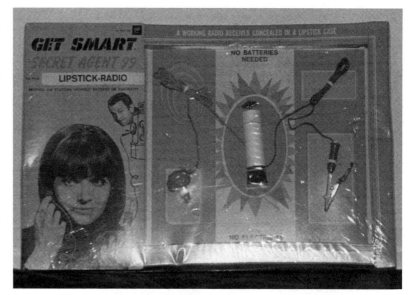

426. GET SMART! COMIC BOOK SERIES
  Dell (1966-1967) *Opposite page*

This three-issue set all have cover photos of Don Adams.

Issue #1	*VG to Mint*	*$65-$70*
Issue #2	*VG to Mint*	*$45*
Issue #3	*VG to Mint*	*$40*

427. GET SMART! AGENT 99 SPY PURSE
  Miner (1965) *Not illustrated*

For the young female viewers of the show, this was a convenient depository for Agent 99's Lipstick Radio.

VG to Mint $80-$90

428. GET SMART! COLORING BOOK
  Saalfield (1965) *Not illustrated*

This book can be really valuable if no one has colored in it!

VG to Mint $50-$60

429. GET SMART! SUNBEAM CAR MODEL
  AMT (1968) *Not illustrated*

A late entry into the GET SMART! collectibles arena, this plastic replica of Maxwell Smart's sports car has become a pricey item.

Mint in Box $350-$400

430. GET SMART! FRAME TRAY PUZZLE
  Jaymar (1966) *Not illustrated*

Another 'smart' addition to a spy toys collection, this puzzle came with a tray to hold the pieces.

VG to Mint $60-$75

431. GET SMART! MINI BOARD GAME
  Ideal (1966) *Not illustrated*

A neat cartoon drawing on the box lid makes this a great display piece.

Good to Mint $60-$75

432. GET SMART! SUPER SLATE
  Saalfield (1966) *Not illustrated*

"Would you believe..." what this item is worth?

Good to Mint $75-$100

Secret Agent

(1965-1966)   CBS Network

This show was a British import and was a re-packaged version of the series English program DANGERMAN.

The thinking man's spy show, it starred Patrick McGoohan as Agent John Drake. The title song "Secret Agent Man" become a big hit.

For such a terrific show, it had a surfeit of collectibles.

As a footnote, McGoohan was offered the role of James Bond on two occasions. He declined both times. Also, although it was never "officially" stated, the secret agent character of John Drake continued into McGoohan's next series, the cult favorite THE PRISONER.

433.   JOHN DRAKE SECRET AGENT GAME
Milton-Bradley (1966) *Not illustrated*

A colorful painting of John Drake in action decorates the lid of this board game.

VG to Mint $40-$50

434.   SECRET AGENT CRASH-MOBILE
Tri-Play (1965) *Not illustrated*

A bumper-car toy... an odd choice for a show that avoided car chases and traditional spy tales.

Mint $90-$100

435.   SECRET AGENT GOLDEN SNIPER GUN
Crescent (1965) *Not illustrated*

A neat gun and a rare collectible to locate. Guess this makes John Drake the original "Man with the Golden Gun!"

VG to Mint $175-$200

436.   SECRET AGENT COMIC BOOK SET
Gold Key (1966-1968) *Above*

Only two comics were ever produced. Both had nice color photos from the show.

Issue #1	*Mint*	*$65-$75*
Issue #2	*Mint*	*$45-$50*

Mission: Impossible

(1966-1973)   CBS Network

One of the all-time classic television series, it failed in only one mission: to produce a good selection of toys and collectibles.

Your mission, if you decide to accept it: locate these hard to find items for your spy toys collection.

437.   MISSION: IMPOSSIBLE VIEWMASTER SET
GAF (1968) *Not illustrated*

A three-reel, 3-D adventure, specially shot on the MISSION: IMPOSSIBLE sets for Viewmaster.

Mint in Package $40-$50

438.   MISSION: IMPOSSIBLE BOARD GAME
Berwick (1975) *Not illustrated*

A relatively common and fairly inexpensive piece, now would be a good time to snap one up.

Good to Mint $20-$30

439.   MISSION: IMPOSSIBLE TV BOOK
Whitman (1969) *Not illustrated*

The adaption, called "The Priceless Particle", is hardly that. But it makes a good collectible.

Mint $8-$10

440.   MISSION: IMPOSSIBLE BOOK SERIES
Popular Library (1967-1969) *Above*

Four paperbacks, each with a photo cover, were released over two years. Each is valued the same.

VG to Mint $10-$15

441.   MISSION : IMPOSSIBLE BOARD GAME
Ideal (1968) *Not illustrated*

The original MISSION: IMPOSSIBLE board game.

VG To Mint $60-$80

442.   MISSION: IMPOSSIBLE RECORD ALBUM
Dot (1966) *Not illustrated*

Lalo Schifrin's perfect theme song was initially released on this album along with other M.I. melodies.

Good to Mint $20-$25

Other Spy Toy Collectibles

443. THE IPCRESS FILE BOARD GAME
Milton-Bradley (1966) *Left, top*

The only collectible made for this film. The cover features Michael Caine as Harry Palmer.

Mint in Box $40-$50

444. THE IPCRESS FILE RECORD ALBUM
Decca (1965) *Not illustrated*

With a great score by John Barry, this album is long out of print.

Mint (unpunched) $75

445. BILLION DOLLAR BRAIN RECORD ALBUM
United Artists (1968) *Left, bottom*

The last Harry Palmer caper, with a score by Richard Rodney Bennett, has a pop-art album cover.

Mint (unpunched) $20-$25

446. OUR MAN FLINT PAPERBACK BOOK
IN LIKE FLINT PAPERBACK BOOK
Pocket Books (1965 and 1966) *Not illustrated*

A double-shot of agent Derek Flint's adventures.

VG to Mint $5-$8

447. OUR MAN FLINT RECORD ALBUM
20th Century-Fox (1966) *Left, center*

Artwork from the movie poster apppears on this disc cover, making it an attractive display piece. Great music by Jerry Goldsmith.

Mint (unpunched) $30-$40

448. IN LIKE FLINT RECORD ALBUM
20th Century-Fox (1967) *Not illustrated*

Collectible, but not as popular (or valuable) as the first.

Mint (unpunched) $25-$35

Spy Toy TV Commercials

With television of the mid-Sixties populated by so many spy shows, what better way to sell spy toys than by advertising on them?

That's exactly what companies like A.C. Gilbert, Mattel, Marx, Topper and American Character did to promote their lines of secret agent spythings.

Those TV commercials were crude by today's flashy computer-generated standards. But these 60-second bits of pop nostalgia were very persuasive in enticing kid spies to get their parents to buy them the latest toy featuring their favorite undercover agent. There were also generic spy toys like Mattel's Zero-M or Topper's Secret Sam.

The same children who watched spy shows in prime time watched Saturday morning cartoon shows like THE BEATLES, SECRET SQUIRREL and COOL McCOOL. Advertisements for spy toys ran heavily in these types of programs.

The following pages have a few examples of these early spy toy TV commercials.

Secret Sam Spy Attache Case
1965 Television Commercial

Topper Toys produced this 60-seceond black-and-white commercial to advertise SECRET SAM, a spy attache case with numerous devices. The filmmakers tried to give the commercial a tense feeling with lots of tight shots and percussive music.

ANNOUNCER:

Topper Toys, makers of SECRET SAM, with hidden camera that really works!

OFF CAMERA VOICE: (whispering)

Your Assignment: DANGER.
Mission: Find the Master Spy.
The Weapon: SECRET SAM.

ANNOUNCER:

Through SECRET SAM'S Mirror Scope, you see him but he can't see you.

You locate the Master Spy. You talk to him. And SECRET SAM'S Hidden Camera is taking his picture right now!

Suddenly, you're discovered!

SECRET SAM fires bullets from inside the case. SECRET SAM has barrel extension. Special missile sends message to your partner.

Mission accomplished!

You hand over real photograph. SECRET SAM with Periscope, Message Missile, Rifle Stock, Barrel Extension. Even shoots through carrying case. And this real camera that works, in secretly... or out. Takes real photos.

OFF CAMERA VOICE: (whispering)

SECRET SAM. SECRET SAM.

James Bond Secret Pen and Vapor Paper
1965 Television Commercial

American Character sold several James Bond toys in 1965. This 60-second black-and-white commercial was shot in shadow, and two voice-over actors with phony English accents played an impatient Q and an amazed Bond. The Bond voice sounded nothing like Sean Connery!

Q:

Sit down, Bond.
Here: the 007 Ring.

JAMES BOND:

It leaves the 007 seal!

Q:

The 007 I.D. Bracelet. Conceals ammunition and message pellets for use with the 007 Pen.

An ordinary pen, isn't it?
Writes like one. But it projects messages over 20 feet.

JAMES BOND:

Ingenious!

Q:

And should you find yourself trapped, you merely whistle for help. *(sound of whistle.)*

Then, by placing ammunition in that slot... *(sound of loud click)*
Careful, Bond!

This is Vapor Paper.
Writing messages to our agents. Drop it in water...

JAMES BOND:

Astonishing!

Q:

Good luck, Bond. You're on your own.

ANNOUNCER:

Get your 007 Secret Agent Pen and Disappearing Vapor Paper separately, or packaged with a 007 Secret Agent Ring and I.D. Bracelet.

You'll get a bang out of it. By American Character.

Zero M Sonic Blaster
1965 Television Commercial

A young Kurt Russell starred in this this 1965 black-and-white 60-second TV commercial for Mattel's Zero M Sonic Blaster. The weapon shot an intense blast of air at targets that came with the gun. William Conrad (radio voice of Gunsmoke's Matt Dillon and later TV's CANNON) supplied the deep voice-over.

(Tense Mission: Impossible-type music)

ANNOUNCER:

You must not fail, Zero M.

This mission is critical.

(Boy takes aim at Goldfinger-like factory.)

This is a most unusual weapon.

It is specially designed for counter espionage.

For Agent Zero M.

It's called the Zero M Sonic Blaster.

This is why:

It fires a massive blast of compressed air and this tremendous roar is the actual sound.

(Loud roar.)

For training purposes this special delayed-action target comes with it.

OFF CAMERA VOICE:

Get Mattel's powerful Zero M Sonic Blaster.

Wherever toys are sold.

(Lowers voice)
Remember the password:

Zero M.

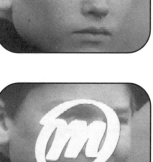

SPY TOYS

as featured in the

Sears, Roebuck & Co.
1965-1967
Christmas Wishbooks

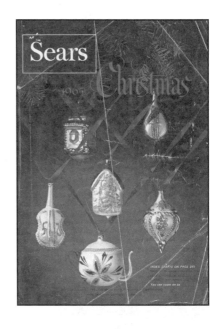

James Bond 007 🔫

Featuring an authentic model of his customized

NEW Modular Construction . . .
only 6 sections to assemble

JAMES BOND 007 ROAD RACE

1965

Road Race..

Aston Martin DB5

Varied-speed
motor sounds
Bullet shield
Tire "cutters"
"Machine guns"

Roar from LeMans start into double-exit tunnel .. which route will your car take?

Danger! Use your skill to zig-zag over winding road, spin around an oil slick

Fly past warning lights and make dare-devil leap over "washed-out" bridge

Hug the banked curve, then climb up the 40° steep hill with its "slippery bricks"

plus ..

Amazingly realistic roads that wind through majestic scenery .. lap counters, switches, even 3 flashing lights at danger points

Assemble it in just minutes

Slide together 6 fully landscaped, fully wired, fully contoured tiles. Strong 4-prong "trees" lock them in place. Even the power pack hides under a hill. Each tile 17x17 inches, colorful injection-molded plastic.

COMPLETE SET
includes 51x34-inch roadway, 2 cars, speed controls and power pack

$34⁴⁴

James Bond's "Aston Martin" parks next to a Mustang Fastback. A scuffle, then a "shot." The Mustang roars off, James Bond follows in pursuit. Into the tunnel with surprise exits .. one car takes the short zig-zag route, the other a long "S" curve. Spin past an oil slick and 2 banked curves. Climb the hill (the slippery bricks look treacherous). Wind around the mountain .. a flashing warning light—bridge "washed out". Both cars chance it—and make it (span adjusts to 4 positions as skill increases). Will James Bond catch his quarry? It's up to you—and your daring.

Set has 3-dimensional roadway, two 3⅝-inch motorized plastic cars, 2 controls, 12-volt power pack. UL listed. 110-120-v. 60-c. AC. 79 N 7666L—Shipping weight 15 lbs. $34.44

Extra Cars to interchange with cars in set. Sturdy plastic. 3⅝ in. long. Wt. each 4 oz.
49 N 7667—Jaguar XK-E............$2.99
49 N 7668—Ferrari 250 GTO........ 2.99

Spare Parts Kit. Contains 2 tires, pick-ups, 1 front guide pin, gear plate, axle face gear.
49 N 7669—Shpg. wt. 3 oz.........Kit 99c

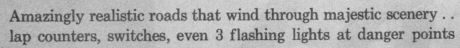

No Money Down on anything Sears sells

PCBKMA
EDSLG SEARS 447

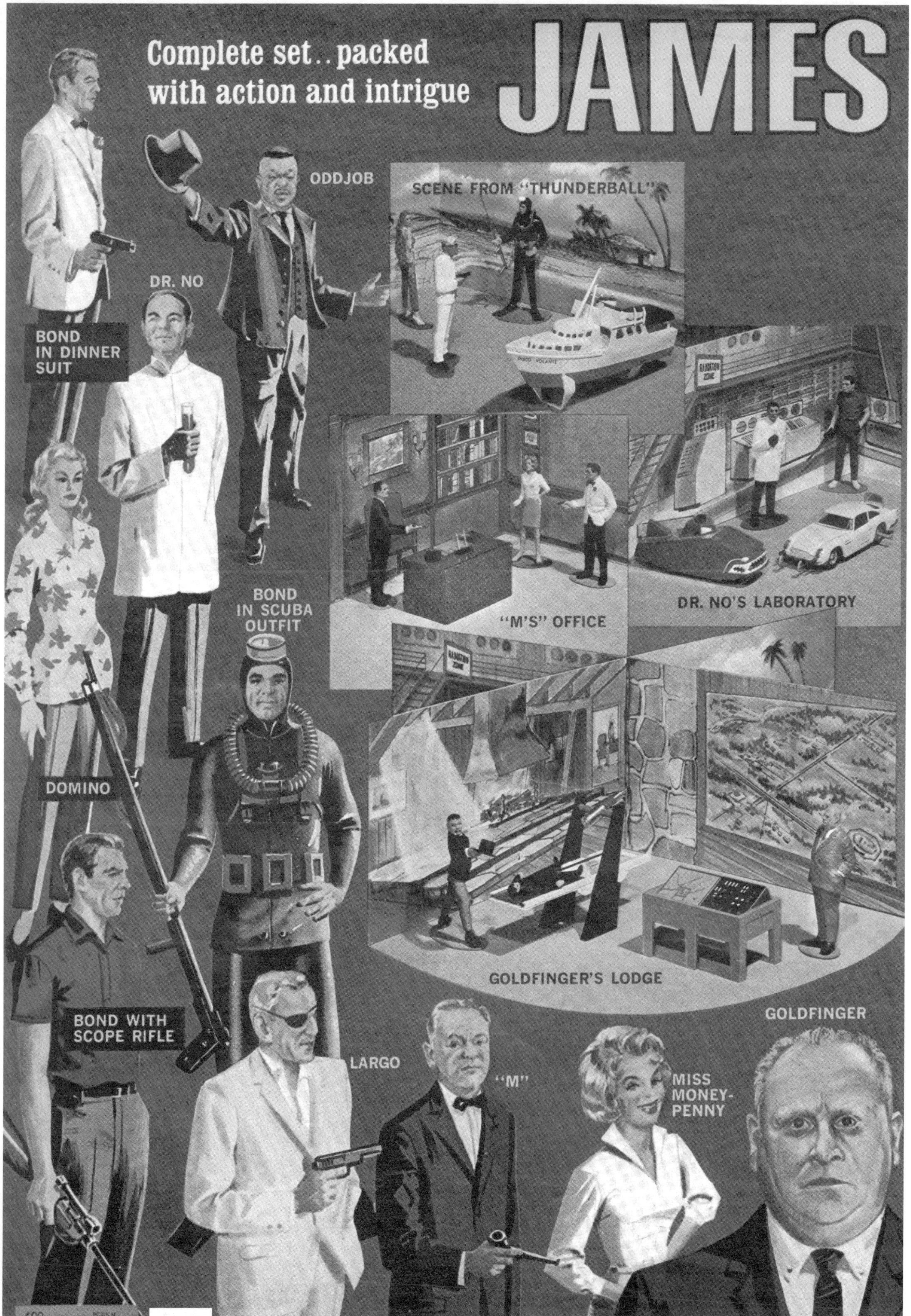
Complete set.. packed with action and intrigue
JAMES
ODDJOB
SCENE FROM "THUNDERBALL"
DR. NO
BOND IN DINNER SUIT
"M'S" OFFICE
DR. NO'S LABORATORY
BOND IN SCUBA OUTFIT
DOMINO
GOLDFINGER'S LODGE
BOND WITH SCOPE RIFLE
GOLDFINGER
LARGO
"M"
MISS MONEY-PENNY
490 SEARS

1965

BOND
and the world of 007

Get a realistic 4-scene stage, 10 lifelike handcolored figures —plus all these working units:

1. Laser-beam Torture Machine
2. Flame-shooting Dragon Tank
3. M's bulletproof Office Desk
4. Revolving-top Pool Table
5. Customized Aston-Martin Car
6. Two-section Hydrofoil Yacht

Everything to recreate Bond's most thrilling adventures

All this for only **$9⁹⁹**

Help James Bond challenge ruthless villains and their cunning gadgets. Every item authentically reproduced from actual settings and characters in his 4 great movies: "From Russia with Love," "Dr. No," "Goldfinger," and his latest—"Thunderball."

With orders from M, head of British counterspies, 007 uses car, scuba gear or other means to get to each villain's hideout. There he must face fiendish machines. But your cleverness lends a hand—and Bond soon turns the tables on the bad guys (hurray!). 22x22x5½-in. stage. Plastic units, 3¼-in. figures.
49 N 5980—Shipping wt. 3 lbs. 8 oz.... Set $9.99

LASER MACHINE
..spring-powered slab moves Bond towards the deadly "ray"

DRAGON TANK
..spews out plastic flames when you press the turret

M's DESK
..bulletproof "glass" goes up to protect Britain's top agent

FLIPS

"DISCO VOLANTE" YACHT
..drops stern section for fast getaway on hydrofoils

POOL TABLE
..top flips over to control panel and map of Fort Knox

ASTON-MARTIN CAR
..bullet shield rises, license plate rotates

BLAST 'EM
with the Zero M
SONIC BLASTER

WHAM

by Mattel

Bursts of air travel up to 40 feet to knock down airport "buildings" $6.99

Pump the handle, aim and pull trigger . . watch toy buildings scatter as a harmless blast of air knocks down your target. High-impact plastic and metal gun, 35 inches long, features a working sight for precision aiming. Cardboard enemy airport features spectacular triple delayed-reaction "explosion" when hit by a blast of air.
79 N 2617C—Shipping weight 5 pounds.....................$6.99

Golden Agent Pistol Set $2.97

Cap-firing .38 made of die-cast gold-color metal. Mount barrel extension, silencer and scope for long-range "firing." Leather belt with holster for silencer and extension. Secret, palm-size cap-firing .45 pistol in tuck-away holster attached to belt chain for quick draws.
49 N 2846—Shpg. wt. 2 lbs. 8 oz.....$2.97

It's a radio—
Now a rifle

Zero M Radio-Rifle $2.62

Looks like a portable radio, but when danger lurks: turn it "on," stock and barrel spring out into a 19-in. plastic rifle that fires caps. Shpg. wt. 1 lb. 1 oz.
49 N 2629.......$2.62

It's a camera—
Now a pistol

Zero M Snap-Shot $1.62

Looks like an ordinary camera, but when you "see" danger—press shutter . . barrel and pistol grip pop out, fires caps. Plastic. Shpg. wt. 8 oz.
49 N 2627.......$1.62

RAA-TAT-TAT

The ISA 07-11 Gun, Holster Set $2.88

Pull plastic burp gun trigger for fast firing—hear rat-ta-tat machine gun sound. 19-inch burp gun. Cap-firing hand gun shoots caps and plastic bullets. Hide small pistol in shoulder holster with strap. With badge and wallet.
49 N 2691G—Shpg. wt. 2 lbs. 12 oz..$2.88
Not for sale in Massachusetts or New York City

RAA-TAT-TAT

Zero M Night-Fighter $2.66

Bolt-action machine gun features an adjustable "infra-red" scope, smoking barrel with "silencer/flash hider." Fires caps singly or in bursts. Plastic, 27 in. long.
79 N 2621C—Shipping weight 2 pounds.......$2.66

DING   DING

Bull's eye flashes, bell rings as you shoot bullets of light
ELECTRONIC RIFLE RANGE NOW WITH PISTOL

Complete set $14.95 without batteries

Big 35-inch rifle and 7-inch pistol both trigger a beam of light with precision accuracy. 1½-foot high target has spring-motorized wand with photo-electric bull's eye. 4 wild-animal heads snap on wand to vary the "game." Score cards. Plastic weapons and target. Order all 3 batteries below.
79 N 2708LM—Shipping wt. 10 lbs. Set $14.95

"D" Battery. Order 6 for target only.
79 N 4660—Shpg. wt. ea. 4 oz.....Each 16c; 6 for 90c
79 N 2670M—9-v. Battery for rifle. Wt. 5 oz. Each $1.49
79 N 6417M—9-v. Battery for pistol. Wt. 4 oz. Each 35c

1965

No International Secret Agent would <u>dare</u> be without his

ISA 07-11 ATTACHÉ CASE

Luger shoots caps and harmless bullets, has easily attached "silencer"
. . converts into burp gun with grenade launcher and sight 'em "scope" **$3⁸⁸**

Plastic attaché case measures 14x9 inches and holds everything you'll need to capture a spy. The gun is there. Bullets, too. Mount shoulder rod extension and long barrel, put on "telescopic-like" sight and you've a weapon that extends to 26 inches. Luger has now become a burp gun and fires a cap-exploding rifle grenade and a missile to carry messages. Cap-exploding hand grenade also in case with key-operated booby trap. Kit of metal and plastic.
49 N 2692G—Shipping wt. 2 lbs. 14 oz. (Not sold in N.Y.C., Mass.). Kit $3.88

Save this catalog . . you can order toys on page 441 to 673 until Sept. 1, 1966

Innocent-looking Secret Agent's Outfit $7⁹⁷

Case explodes	Bullets fly	Hidden Dagger
Code Book booby-trapped	Hidden Pocket Secret Wallet	Secret Message Coding Machine

007 reporting, sir. Yes, I'm ready, I have my attaché case with my rifle (it's a pistol as well as a rifle, you know.) I'll keep my assignment in the booby-trap code book that fires a cap when opened by the wrong person. I'll send you a full report with my Code-O-Matic secret message writer. I've got my wallet, passport, foreign money. Jolly good, sir. Case 17x12 in.
49 N 2727G—Shpg. wt. 4 lbs. (Not sold in N.Y.C., Mass.).$7.97

Uses #127 film

Secret Sam Snooper Gun
Includes Attaché Case with secret Camera $6⁸⁸

Track a spy—take his picture with secret camera in or out of case. Check scene with periscope. Mount silencer, fire play bullets. Put on rifle stock and barrel to shoot secret message missile. Case 15x11½ in.
49 N 2694—Shipping weight 4 pounds. $6.88

Multi-Pistol 09

See enemy thru the scope. Fire play bullets long or short range. Mount barrel extension to fire "exploding" grenade, cap-firing torpedo bomb, secret message missile, armor-piercing rocket. Derringer, hidden in handle, pops out, fires caps. Shipping weight 2 lbs. 4 oz.
49 N 2696. . . . . $3.44

$3⁴⁴

THE MAN FROM **U.N.C.L.E.** NAPOLEON SOLO GUN

$3⁶⁶

Two-way gun fires clip-loaded caps

Cap-shooting .45 converts to long-range rifle

Solo may go it alone, but never without his gun. Automatic pistol becomes a 29-in. long rifle when you mount barrel, shoulder stock and extension "silencer." Scope has crosshairs. Rugged metal and plastic.
49 N 2709G—Shpg. wt. 1 lb. 8 oz. (Not sold in N.Y.C.) . . . . Kit $3.66

NOTE: *Caps not included with any cap-firing toy.*

1965

James Bond and Oddjob meet again!

11-inch action figures complete with fabric clothes

Secret Agent 007 actually swings out right arm to shoot cap-firing pistol . . kicks out knife-wielding foot.

Oddjob throws his steel-rimmed top hat . . executes a deadly karate stroke.

Cap-firing gun stores inside case

James Bond *plus* weapons attaché case

$6⁹⁹

You want action . . you get action with this authentic model of Sean Connery as James Bond. Available only at Sears.
007 is licensed to "rub out" evil villains. Just press his right arm down . . *Crack!* Fast reflex aims gun and shoots a bullet-sounding cap (not incl.). Push his right leg back . . *Swish!* Sudden kick springs out harmless knife.
Detailed jointed plastic. Dressed in business suit with shirt, tie. Pack away gun in secret pocket or plastic attaché case.
49 N 5981—Shipping wt. 1 lb.. . . .$6.99

Extra Outfits for James Bond

$2⁹⁹ to $3⁹⁹

007 must dress right when he's on different assignments. Impeccably tailored fabrics. You'll find his size only at Sears. No figures. Shipping weight each 8 ounces.

49 N 5986—**Summer Formal.** Tuxedo coat and pants, shirt, bow tie $3.99

49 N 5985—**Sports Outfit.** Casual knit shirt, slacks. Telescopic rifle $2.99

49 N 5984—**Commander Outfit.** Navy dress jacket, trousers, shirt, tie. . . .$3.99

Oddjob . . Goldfinger's fearsome handyman

$6⁹⁹

"Perhaps the most dangerous animal on the face of the earth," James Bond said in awe. "Be especially wary if he removes his hat." Oddjob gleefully obeys orders. Push his right arm in towards body . . *Whang!* He flings his hat sideways like a boomerang. Pull his left arm up . . *Whack!* His forearm chops downward like an axe. Authentically detailed just like the movie version. Plastic figure comes dressed in a cutaway formal suit with rigid plastic hat.
49 N 5982—Shipping weight 1 lb.. . . . .$6.99

"Charge it" if you wish

492 SEARS PCBK 8 AEOSLG

1965

Clue $2⁹⁷

You're the sleuth in this challenging detective game to discover the who, where and how of the crime. Use the clue cards to find the answers and enjoy a new plot every time. Weapons, notes included. Intrigue for 3 to 6 players, ages 8 to adult.
49 N 390—Shipping weight 2 lbs. 8 oz.......$2.97

Mystic Skull $3⁸⁴

Skull dances on end of limb, then stops. The idea's to put "hex" on the other fellow by sticking pins in his voodoo doll. To win, just keep some pinholes in your doll open. Board, bone stirrer, tokens, dolls combine to tingle the spines of 2-4 players.
49 N 232—Shipping weight 2 pounds.......$3.84

Addams Family Game $1⁶⁶

Time for the annual Addams family midnight picnic in the cemetery, but nobody's there. Horrors! That's why you must round up 4 of them in front of their beautiful mansion to win this game. 2 to 4 players shouldn't find the obstacles *too* eerie.
49 N 395—Shipping weight 1 lb. 12 oz.......$1.66

Combat $1⁵²

You're in command in this big battle, and it's a challenge to keep your men free while capturing 6 enemy soldiers. Your men have to occupy his headquarters to do it. Spin to see who captures or escapes. 12 soldiers, cards, board. 2 play. Ages 7 to 14.
49 N 297—Shipping weight 1 lb. 12 oz.......$1.52

$1³²

You actually race the clock in this high-spying James Bond game of strategy. Place your 3 men carefully, score with each "spy"

As an agent of James Bond, start mission from points you select on board. Now plan your moves. Gather spy cards, maneuver men, advance scoring disks. "Rendezvous" can mean extra points. First one to score 100 points is winner. 2 to 4 "agents" can play. Thrilling intrigue; for ages 10 up.
49 N 402—Shpg. wt. 1 lb. 12 oz......$1.32

Get "Hot Tip" clues
.. track down agents
Agent Zero M Spy Detector
$3³²

The secret Rocket Fuel formula is gone. You'll be Top Secret Agent and win the game if you can unmask the thief. It's easy, exciting. Spy Detector, cards, scoreboard help you analyze clues and testimony of the 24 witness suspects. For 2 to 4 rather deductive agents.
49 N 221—Shpg. wt. 1 lb. 12 oz....$3.32

*Just call Sears
and say "Charge It"*

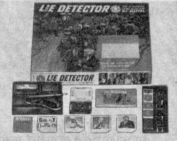

Man from U.N.C.L.E. $2²²

Clever as Napoleon Solo? You'll thrill to challenge of being first to find THRUSH chief card that matches your assignment card and returning it to U.N.C.L.E. headquarters. Turns 2-4 players into U.N.C.L.E. agents.
49 N 403—Shpg. wt. 1 lb. 12 oz......$2.22

Lie Detector $3⁷²

Scene: a TV studio. Crime: serious and unsolved. You: 1 of 2 to 4 sleuths trying to go from detective to Chieftain by accumulating facts and suspects to nail the culprit. And only the Lie Detector knows truth of it all.
49 N 193—Shpg. wt. 1 lb. 12 oz......$3.72

Who would think you're an International Secret Agent carrying a booby-trapped 18-piece arsenal

ISA 07-II ATTACHÉ CASE $3.99

Luger shoots caps and harmless bullets, has easily attached "silencer" .. converts into burp gun with grenade launcher and sight 'em "scope"

Attaché case looks innocent enough, but it holds everything you need on a dangerous mission. The gun is there. Bullets, too. Mount shoulder rod extension and long barrel with "telescopic-like" sight. Luger has now become a 26-inch burp gun that launches a cap-exploding rifle grenade or a missile to carry messages. When outnumbered, cap-exploding hand grenade evens the odds. 14x9-inch case has key-operated booby trap. Plastic and metal.
49 N 2692G—Shipping wt. 3 lbs. (Not sold in N.Y.C.)........Kit $3.99

Save this catalog .. you can order toys on pages 467 to 638 until August 1, 1967.

JAMES BOND SECRET AGENT 007
Special Assignment Set

3 targets

$3.49

Only Sears outfits agents with this low priced set

You must eliminate 3 enemy agents, 007. Your kit has a pistol that automatically fires soft plastic bullets when you attach the scope. Add shoulder stock for 18-in. rifle. Booby-trap code book and "radio" fire caps. Calling cards. Plastic, metal. Not sold in N.Y.C.
49 N 2707G—Wt. 2 lbs. Set $3.49

Code book

"Radio"

007 B.A.R.K.
Bond Assault Raider Kit
$5.88

James Bond's most devastating weapon converts from a businessman's case to an all-out attack arsenal. Built-in launcher lobs 3 harmless rockets. Pistol shoots a message-carrying missile or cap-exploding grenade .. also conceals cap-firing palm gun. 14x11-in. case shoots, too. Plastic, metal.
Shpg. wt. 2 lbs. 3 oz.
49 N 2712..........Kit $5.88

International Secret Agent Submachine Gun

Pull back bolt for rapid-fire action. Ring sight lifts up .. cross-hairs center spy's silhouette. Squeeze trigger .. it fires bursts, muzzle recoils. 21-inch gun-blue plastic, metal parts.
49 N 2674—Wt. 2 lbs... $2.39

$2.39

Man from U.N.C.L.E. "It's a THRUSH Rifle"

See pop-up targets

$6.29

Fires magazine clip-loaded caps

Targets pop up in sniper-scope .. bam! They drop

Hefty 36-inch THRUSH rifle is quite a wonder. Its ray-sight zooms in on daytime danger with crosshair accuracy. For simulated night fighting, a flick of the side switch sets up 4 deadly targets—right in the sight. Pull trigger—the target vanishes in a blast of crackling cap fire. Load caps in magazine clip. Plastic, metal.
79 N 2699L—Shipping weight 3 pounds..................$6.29

Man from U.N.C.L.E. Napoleon Solo Gun

$3.99

Fires magazine clip-loaded caps

Cap-shooting .45 converts to a long-range rifle

Automatic pistol becomes a 27-inch long rifle when you mount barrel, shoulder stock and extension "silencer." Scope has calibrated cross-hairs. Load caps in magazine clip. Rugged plastic with metal parts. Why not pick up the phone and order it?
49 N 2709G—Shpg. wt. 1 lb. 8 oz. (Not sold in N.Y.C.).... $3.99
NOTE for both pages: Caps not included with any cap-firing toy.

1966

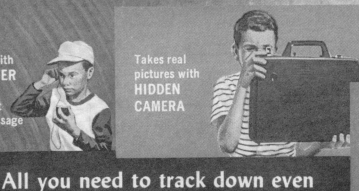

It's U.N.C.L.E. vs. THRUSH!

Blast sinister THRUSH agents off rooftops of giant 54x17½-in. set—before your opponent can wipe out the crime-fighting men from U.N.C.L.E.

23-piece set $3⁹⁹ A Sears Exclusive

Who are better marksmen .. the men from U.N.C.L.E. or agents of Thrush? Find out fast. Hook together colorful 3-section set of heavy cardboard. Then players position their 5½-inch plastic men .. grab their dart pistols .. and start firing. First one to knock down all his opponent's men wins. 2 pistols, 6 rubber-tipped darts, 2 grenades.
79 N 306C—Shipping weight 4 pounds...................$3.99

Twelve, 5½-inch figures, including ..

Illya Kuryakin

Alexander Waverly

Napoleon Solo

$3⁹⁹

Shoot powerful bursts of air at stationary animal target —or fire away at moving bubbles

Needs no ammunition .. cock lever and pull trigger. If you hit target, vinyl wildcat scene will ripple. Also knock bubbles out of air .. magic liquid and wand included. 30-in. heavy gauge steel rifle, wood-grained plastic stock. 27x9-in. target. Use your phone if you want to order it the easiest way of all.
79 N 307C—Shpg. wt. 3 lbs.......$3.99

BLAM

Send a giant jet of air across the room with a hurricane-action Air Blaster Gun

$4⁷⁹

When you bulls-eye the snarling gorilla target, he jumps, shakes and quivers .. vinyl strands re-form for more. You get 4 outer space targets, too. No ammunition needed .. harmless as a breeze. Hinged hand-lever on top builds air pressure. Sturdy, 10-in. black plastic gun. 12x21-in. targets. Shipping weight 1 lb. 7 oz.
49 N 2666...................Set $4.79

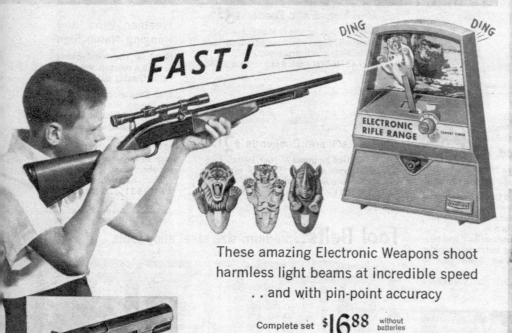

FAST !

DING DING

ELECTRONIC RIFLE RANGE

These amazing Electronic Weapons shoot harmless light beams at incredible speed .. and with pin-point accuracy

Complete set $16⁸⁸ without batteries

Practice firing big 35-inch rifle. When you think you've reached "sharp-shooter" standing .. switch over to pistol for toughest challenge of all. 1½-foot high target has spring-motorized wand with photo-electric bull's eye that flashes and rings when you hit it. Four wild animal heads snap on wand to vary the "game." Plastic weapons and target. Scorecards included. Order all three batteries below.
79 N 2708LM—Shipping weight 10 pounds*..............Set $16.88
79 N 4660—"D" Battery. Order 6 for target. Wt. 4 oz..Ea. 16c; 6 for 90c
79 N 2670M—9-v. Battery. Order 1 for rifle. Wt. 5 oz...Each $1.49
79 N 6417M—9-v. Battery. Order 1 for pistol. Wt. 4 oz......Each 35c

*Allow 10 lbs. postage per postal regulations

You also get 7-in. .45 pistol to really test your skill

$2⁹⁵

Batman Target Arcade

Shoot at long-time enemies of those fearless crime fighters, Batman and Robin .. or knock over the 5 panels in front of them. Self-loading plastic pistol fires metal pellets. Nose of pistol attached to frame. Plastic canopy. Metal legs. Abt. 20x11½x7 in.high.
49 N 185—Shpg. wt. 5 lbs. 4 oz....$2.95

1966

Save this catalog. You can order toys on pages 467 to 638 from now until August 1, 1967

James Bond

.. pull back arm of 11-in. figure, it springs forward, pistol fires cap **$2⁹⁹**

1 Agent 007 comes right out of "Thunderball" in trunks, pullover shirt, scuba mask, snorkel, fins. Die-cast metal Beretta fires caps (caps not incl.) Plastic figure.
49 N 59801—Shipping weight 6 ounces............$2.99

Outfit your James Bond action figure in these "Thunderball" creations

2 The Jump Jet. Bond uses rockets to "fly" over walls and buildings. Tommy gun fires caps (caps not incl.). Shirt, pants and shoes. From Japan.
49 N 59804—Shipping weight 4 ounces....................$2.39

3 Disguise Kit. 2 different masks, cap-firing hand grenade (without caps). Trench coat, dark glasses, binoculars. Pants, shoes and hat. From Japan.
49 N 59802—Shipping weight 4 ounces....................$2.99

4 Scuba Outfit. Scuba vehicle, fins, spear gun that fires projectiles, air tanks, scuba jacket. Headpiece with detachable duck decoy. From Japan.
49 N 59803—Shipping weight 4 ounces.....................$2.99

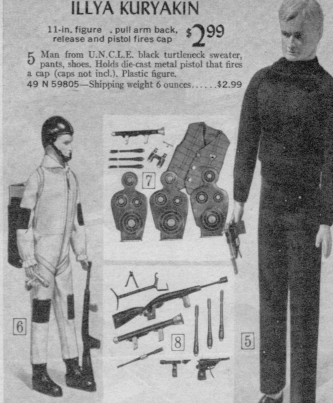

ILLYA KURYAKIN

11-in. figure . pull arm back, release and pistol fires cap **$2⁹⁹**

5 Man from U.N.C.L.E. black turtleneck sweater, pants, shoes. Holds die-cast metal pistol that fires a cap (caps not incl.). Plastic figure.
49 N 59805—Shipping weight 6 ounces......$2.99

Illya's ready for "THRUSH" when he wears these outfits

6 Jump Suit Set. Boots and helmet with chin strap. Parachute and pack. Cap-firing Tommy gun (without caps) with telescopic sight.
49 N 59807—From Japan. Shipping weight 4 ounces.........$2.99

7 Target Set. Bulletproof vest, 3 targets with stands, spring-firing bazooka that fires 3 shells, binoculars for sighting "THRUSH"
49 N 59806—From Japan. Shipping weight 4 ounces.........$1.89

8 Arsenal Set. Cap-firing Tommy gun, pistol, (without caps), spring-firing bazooka, 3 shells. Bi-pod, sight, rifle butt for pistol.
49 N 59808—From Japan. Shipping weight 4 ounces.........$1.29

BOOM
BOOM

Clip of 4 shells

Mountain Cat Tank fires shells FAST!

Climbs over boulders and out of ditches as few toys can **$9³⁹** without batteries

Right off the proving grounds. Just touch the lever and watch it roll over almost anything and everything. Climb-Action-Traction gets it over humps. Forward and reverse gears. Fires 4 shells automatically. Shatter-resistant plastic. 22½x9¼x8 inches high. Order 4 "D" batteries on page 519. Buy it the easy way—order by phone.
79 N 5744C--Shipping weight 5 pounds............$9.39

Stony is 11½ in. tall and fully jointed

Stony fits in this big **21¾-inch JEEP**

Front end opens to reveal gear

What a buy!
At Sears you get Stony, his Jeep and 36 pieces of equipment

All for only **$6⁹⁹**

Make him salute, sit, hold a rifle. Head, shoulders, elbows, hips, knees are all movable. Olive uniform. Comes with weapons, walkie-talkie, field glasses, K rations and more. Made of plastic.
79 N 6028C—Shpg. wt. 7 lbs...$6.99

FC [Sears] 515

1966

Lost in Space

Helmet plus Remco's Space Ray Gun

$3.97 set
without batteries

ZZZZZAAAP

Offered nowhere in the universe but at Sears

Explore space with helmet that keeps out "cosmic rays" and ray gun that buzzes, flashes beam of light. White plastic helmet sports a blue light reflector, insignia and chin strap. Fits any child. Chrome-color plastic ray gun. 10½ inches long. Turn lens to send red, green, white or yellow signals. Order 2 "C" batteries on page 482.
49 N 2678—Shipping wt. 1 lb. 12 oz..Set $3.97

Mattel's "Lost-in-Space" Roto-Jet Gun

BLAM BLAM

ROTO-JET GUN

$5.57

4-in-1 weapon . . change sections to form rifle, sub-carbine, launcher or pistol—each sends roto-missiles soaring 40 feet

You're "Lost in Space" with TV's Robinson family. But you're ready for any interplanetary danger with a complete range of weapons. Spin out 2 harmless plastic roto-missiles in true trajectory. Hear an unearthly rising-falling sound, startling ram-fire—or silence. Durable plastic with spring mechanisms, whistler, scope. 24 inches long overall.
79 N 2680C—Shipping weight 3 pounds. $5.57

Sight target   Blast it

BLEEP BLEEP BLEEP

$10.66
without batteries

Transistorized Plazer Ray Gun shoots a beam of light at any target . . "destroys" it in a flash

Sight any object on the wide inner screen. Pull trigger . . hear "bleep" as ray in 1 of 3 colors streaks towards target. Squeeze cap-firing trigger to produce explosive crak! See harmless white flash on screen.

Plastic, metal . . 27 inches long. Filter simulates nighttime firing. Buy 2 "D" batteries below.
79 N 2719C—Wt- 4 lbs. $10.66
"D" Battery. Shpg. wt. ea. 4 oz.
79N4660—Each 16c; 6 for 90c

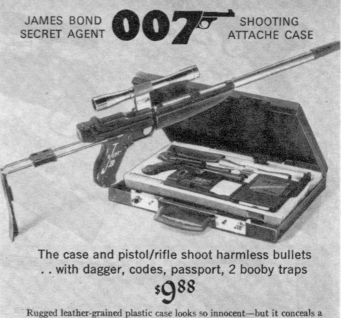

JAMES BOND SECRET AGENT 007 SHOOTING ATTACHE CASE

The case and pistol/rifle shoot harmless bullets . . with dagger, codes, passport, 2 booby traps

$9.88

Rugged leather-grained plastic case looks so innocent—but it conceals a dagger on side, a trigger on top. Open it, there's a 4-piece weapon that assembles into a 30-inch automatic rifle with cartridge-scope . . it's also an automatic pistol or single-shot Luger. 12 plastic bullets. Includes decoding machine, passport, wallet, currency, calling cards. 17x12-inch case and codebook are booby-trapped . . open 'em wrong and cap fires.
49 N 2727G—Shpg. wt. 3 lbs. 8 oz. (Not sold in N.Y.C.). . . .Set $9.88

A movie camera . . click! A machine gun

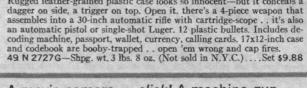

BRRRP

Zero M Movie-Shot

Looks like a camera, pull trigger, barrel pops out. 15-inch plastic gun fires caps in bursts or single shots.
Shipping wt. 1 lb. 12 oz.
49 N 2724. . . . .$3.99

$3.99
New from Mattel

Pocket knife . . click! A pistol

$1.99

Portable radio . . click! A rifle

$3.19

Zero M Pocket-Shot

Looks like a knife, its plastic blade pulls out. Press release . . snaps into 6-in. plastic, metal gun. Fires caps. By Mattel.
49 N 2614—Wt. 8 oz. . . .$1.99

Zero M Radio-Rifle

Looks like a radio, but turn it "on" . . stock and barrel spring out into a 19-inch cap-firing rifle. Plastic, metal. By Mattel.
49 N 2629—Wt. 1 lb. 3 oz. .$3.19

Johnny Seven

RA-TAT-TAT

Johnny Seven One-man Army Weapon $8.33

The only gun in the world that: (1) launches grenade; (2) fires anti-tank rocket; (3) armor-piercing shell; (4) anti-bunker missile; (5) shoots 10 bullets as rifle on bipod; (6) chatters as tommy gun; (7) fires caps as pistol that detaches from gun. Stock also detaches. Magazine-loaded rifle bullets. All ammo big and smooth, made of soft plastic. Highly detailed plastic weapon with metal parts, spring mechanisms. 3 feet long. Made by Topper.
79 N 2754C—Shipping weight 5 pounds. $8.33

Think fast! Push buttons to switch either car to other track .. then get behind and close in

1932 Ford   1931 Duesenberg

$7.95 without batteries

The chase is on! Score points by banging rear bumper of other car .. motorized GETAWAY CHASE GAME

Watch it! The cops are in hot pursuit. To avoid being caught, the bad guys try to sidetrack the police car .. then get behind it. These cops are smart. They *could* sidetrack the Duesenberg. Almost anything can happen when each player controls *both* cars with 4 push buttons. The trick is to *think fast* and out-guess your opponent.

4½-inch plastic cars come fully assembled (each needs 1 "C" battery; order from page 519); two-section plastic layout snaps together .. measures giant-size 32x24 inches wide; 31 unassembled cardboard buildings and trees *plus* 79 pieces of realistic-looking landscaping.
79 N 159L—Shipping weight 5 lbs... Set $7.95

Get out of awful Camp Granada before bus breaks down

$3.88

"Hello Mudda! Hello Fadda! Here we are at Camp Granada!" All the zany fun of Allan Sherman's famous summer camp .. where things are so bad everyone can't wait to get back home. Players collect "icky animals", they carry out tasks, visit Quicksand Beach and Cruddy Creek—but that isn't all. Players must carefully move bus along escape route without radiator dropping out along the way. Loads of fun for 2 to 4 players, ages 6 to 14.
49 N 198—Shipping weight 3 lbs...... $3.88

Carnival fun in Shenanigans $2.39

Test your skill and luck as you travel this exciting midway. First spin the dial to see where you land— could be Palm Reader, Weight Guesser, Snake Charmer or Pie-in-the-Eye. Contests, penalties, surprises. For 2 to 4 players, ages 5 to 12.
49 N 201—Shipping weight 2 lbs........ $2.39

Help Dynamic Duo in Batman $2.39

Gotham City's in the grip of a crime wave. The sinister Riddler .. the cunning Mr. Freeze .. 4 others are in control. Players travel around in Batmobiles searching for them. First one to capture all 6 villains wins. For 2 to 4 players, ages 8 to 15. Like everything else in Sears books, it's so easy to order by telephone.
49 N 236—Shpg. wt. 1 lb. 12 oz....... $2.39

Agent Zero M Spy Detector $3.99

World crisis! Secret rocket fuel formula is stolen. Give witnesses spy detector test .. then discover and accuse guilty spy. Earn promotion every time you spot thief. Rise to Top Secret Agent and win game. Spy detector box, cards, scoreboard help you analyze clues and testimony of 24 witness suspects. For 2 to 4 players, ages 6 to 12.
49 N 252—Shpg. wt. 1 lb. 10 oz...... $3.99

Get Smart with time bomb $2.35

Based on popular TV show starring Don Adams. Players move around game board, taking or rejecting cards, piecing together picture of master criminal. But look out for time bomb—players can set it to blast opponent off board! For 2-4 players, ages 6-12.
49 N 249—Shpg. wt. 1 lb. 12 oz...... $2.35

Man from U.N.C.L.E. $2.39

Clever as Napoleon Solo? Thrill to challenge of being first to find THRUSH chief card that matches your assignment card .. then returning it to U.N.C.L.E. headquarters. For 2 to 4 players, ages 6 to 12.
49 N 403—Shpg. wt. 1 lb. 8 oz....... $2.39

Spy with James Bond $1.66

Face dangers lurking in back alleys, ghostly cemeteries and cavernous sewers. But do your spying before midnight to score high. Gather spy cards, maneuver men, advance scoring disks as you race against time. "Rendevous" can mean extra points. Score 100 points to win. For 2 to 4 players, ages 8 and up.
49 N 402—Shpg. wt. 1 lb. 12 oz...... $1.66

You can talk with a friend and his walkie-talkie up to a mile away

You can pick up CB short wave programs . . . even from ships at sea

You can listen to your favorite local AM radio programs

You can even send wireless code messages

This is a 4-in-1 Communication Unit .. and it is sold exclusively at Sears

Only $29⁵⁰ without batteries

Now your youngster can act like a ham radio operator. He can tune in conversations from the world of action, talk to friends within range by walkie-talkie or telegraph, even listen to music and the latest news. Just turn the on-off volume control knob and tuning knob, then flick 2 switches to transmit or receive, to hear Citizen's Band or AM radio. Transmits over Channel 14 . . receives all CB channels. Switch changes circuitry for AM radio. Solid state circuitry, crystal controlled transmitter-receiver has sensitive variable tuning capacitor. chrome-plated brass an-

tenna that extends 50 inches. Molded plastic cabinet is 16x6x7 inches high with 2½-inch speaker, earphone for private listening. For wireless chats with friends, use another communication unit or any Sears walkie-talkie on these 2 pages. Code booklet incl. From Japan. Uses 6 "D" batteries, not incl. Order 3 packages separately below. Why not pick up the phone and order it?

49 N 6397—Shipping weight 5 lbs. 9 oz. . . . $29.50
"D" Batteries. Package of 2. Shipping weight 8 oz.
49 N 4660. . . . . .Package 36c

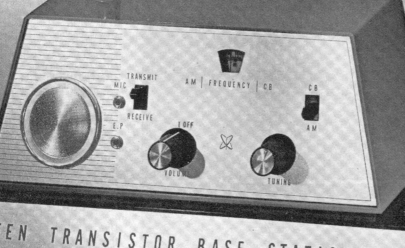

TEN TRANSISTOR BASE STATION

Sears

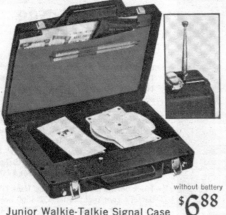

Junior Walkie-Talkie Signal Case with range up to ¼ mile plus code book, passport, "money"

without battery
$6⁸⁸

Super Walkie-Talkie Signal Case

Set includes:
- Walkie-talkie that transmits up to ¼ mile
- Receiver for your pal
- Hidden camera
- 5-power telescope
- Wireless Morse code, light or sun blinker

All this and more!

Only $9⁹⁹ without batteries

Keeps junior secret agents in contact with headquarters or other agents. 3-transistor crystal controlled transmitter and super-regenerative receiver operates on CB Channel 14. Molded plastic case with chrome-plated 40-inch antenna, metal hardware. 10x7½x2 inches deep. Holds big, 2-pocket pouch and accessories. Pencils not included. Uses one 9-volt battery. Order separately below. From Japan. Buy it the easy way—order by phone.
49 N 6391 M—Shipping weight 1 pound 5 ounces. . . .$6.88
49 N 6417 M—9-volt Battery. Shipping weight 4 oz. . . .35c

Also includes buzzer alarm that goes off when opened, Morse code guide, wallet, "money," passport. Your master spy can track down suspect, follow him with telescope, get photographic evidence. His only equipment . . this realistic signal case. Molded plastic, with chrome-plated 40-in. antenna, metal hardware. 4-transistor sends, receives on Channel 14. Transmitter key locks for remote intercom use with removable pocket receiver. Camera uses 127 film (not incl.). With 2-pocket pouch, accessories (pencils not incl.). From Japan. Takes two 9-volt batteries (order separately at left) and one "D" battery (order separately above).
49 N 6392 M—Shipping weight 2 pounds 13 ounces. $9.99

SPY TOYS

as featured in the

Montgomery Ward
1965-1967
Christmas Catalogs

Fun For The Family

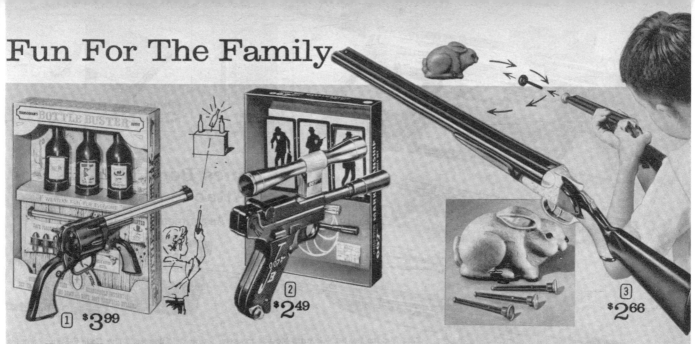

① $3⁹⁹

② $2⁴⁹

③ $2⁶⁶

Bust The Bottles

① Rootin' Tootin' Western-Styled Target for sharp shootin' lawmen. Line "bottles" up in a row and start fanning your pistol. Set 'em up for another round. Three 9-in. plastic bottles "break" apart when hit . . reassemble parts for more action shooting. "Break action" plastic pistol is replica of Colt .45, loads like real gun. Gun has aluminum barrel. 4 harmless plastic bullets. Fun for the whole family.
48 T 756 M—Ship. wt. 2 lbs. 12 oz $3.99

"007" Target

② Secret Agents Train On Similar Type Marksmanship Targets. Use "007" secret agent pistol with silencer and high powered scope or without scope and silencer. Use as a single shot, an automatic pistol. Fires harmless bullets. Target includes 3 plastic-framed hinged targets which fall out of sight when hit and one stationary target. Fun for all potential secret agents.
48 T 843—Ship. wt. 1 lb. 4 oz $2.49

Rabbit Hunt

③ Test Your Skill As A Rabbit Hunter. Wind up rabbit and let him go . . he moves in circles or goes straight which ever way you desire. Test your aim . . see if you can hit him on the run with one of the rubber tipped darts. Motor stops when you knock rabbit down. Children love playing this exciting game. Includes realistic looking mechanical rabbit of sturdy plastic. 23½-in. long double barreled plastic shot gun, shoots one dart or two at a time. 3 harmless suction cup darts. Loads of fun for everyone.
48 T 937 M—Ship. wt. 2 lbs. 8 oz $2.66

④ $3⁹⁹

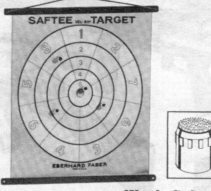

⑤ $1⁹⁹

Soft, safer Velcro sticks like magic— harmless to children

Hands Up Harry

④ Shoot 'Em Up Western Action Game. Hands up Harry automatically responds to direct hits. His hat falls off . . his guns fall out of his hands . . and the final shot brings down his pants (to reveal his bright candy-striped shorts). Plastic western dart gun, 4 suction cup darts included. 28-in. tall masonite target.
48 T 944 M—Ship. wt. 4 lbs. 6 oz $3.99

Wards Saftee Target

⑤ Improve Your Marksmanship With Wards Saftee Target Game. Fun to play. Use it anywhere. High-impact plastic pistol shoots "velcro" tipped bullets. Made of special woven material. Sticks like magic to target only. Will not mar floors and walls or scratch furniture. No points or suction cups. Safer for children of all ages. Fun for adults too! Includes: 14x16-in. target, pistol, 5 velcro tipped bullets.
48 T 700—Shipping weight 10 oz $1.99

⑥ $7⁶⁶

⑦ $1⁶⁹

⑧ $2⁴⁹

Rock 'em Sock 'em Robots

⑥ Work The Controls Of The Robot Fighters. Move them around, throw ferocious right and left punches. It's wild action until one robot connects and knocks the others block off. Push head of robot down, start fight again. 12½-in. high plastic robots move around 20-in. square ring. It's simple for anyone to compete, a real test of skill to win.
48 T 830 M—Ship. wt. 6 lbs. 8 oz $7.66

Skilldrive Road Race

⑦ "Drive It Yourself" by magnetic action control. See if you can maneuver cars around hairpin turns, through tunnels, over bridges. Control cars by wheel and shaft on board. Tests coordination, individual driving skill and judgment. 21 plastic pieces; road blocks, cars, tunnels, bridges. For one or more players of all ages.
48 T 828—Ship. wt. 1 lb. 6 oz $1.69

Wards Speed Demon

⑧ Wards Exclusive 2 Man Stock Car Racing Game. Each player has his own car and track. Magnetic wand controls race cars around curves, pass rock slide, along camel hump ridge, around dead mans curve, through tunnel, up the straightaway. First to complete the circuit wins the race.
48 T 946—Shipping wt.
10 oz $2.49

1965

Old Time Telephone Set
Ivory and Gold French Style Phones $10.00 Set

IMPRESS YOUR GUESTS with the ivory and gold colored French style of your home intercom system. Stylish and practical, turn the crank and the pleasant sounding bell rings on the other end of the line. Operates just like the old ones used to do.

Simple to install, just insert two "D" cells (order below) in each phone and plug in 33-foot wire cord. The sound carries as if you were talking in the same room. Size about 7½ in. tall and 8½ in. wide.
48 HT 20199—Ship. wt. 3 lbs. 1 oz....$10.00

Push-Button Phone Set
$9.66

TRANSISTORIZED TWO-WAY PHONE Set. Looks just like the latest princess-type phones. High-impact plastic, for indoor or outdoor use; transmits voices clearly over 50 feet of connecting wire. Makes a pleasant signal when you press "0" to call other phone. Each bank of push-buttons gives an individual signal tone. Uses 4 "C" cells (order below). See Page 210 for full color picture.
48 HT 20022X–Wt. 3 lbs. 4 oz. $9.66

Hand Phones

[A] BATTERY POWERED INTERCOM for work or play, carries voices clearly over 25 feet of wire. With loud buzzers and 2 wall hangers. 8 in. long. Order 2 "C" cells below. Wt. 1 lb. 2 oz.
48 HT 20048..........$3.77

[B] SECRET TELEPHONE SYSTEM. Voice powered, needs no batteries. Talk from room to room or even house to house without anyone hearing your secrets. Two 8½ in. long plastic phones and 25 feet of wire.
48 HT 20053—Wt. 1 lb. $2.37

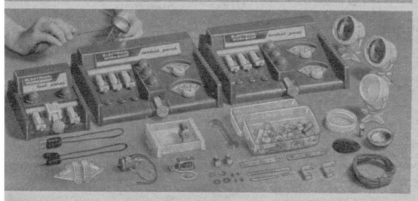

Electric Workshop $6.99

YOUNG ELECTRICAL ENGINEERS will be fascinated by this realistic workshop. Clear instructions explain circuitry, include job sheet for performing electrical experiments. Guide for building a 3-way telegraph system—one station sends, other two-receive. Set contains 2 master control panels, test panel, switches, levers, bulbs, buzzer, bell, testers, electromagnet, wire, telegraph keys, rheostat, electric motor, 3 searchlights, parts box, wrench, screwdriver and other components. High-impact blue plastic with yellow accessories. Order four "C" cells below.
48 HT 20052—Ship. wt. 2 lbs. 8 oz.......$6.99

Ham Radio Broadcast Set $8.50

GOOD INTRODUCTION TO HAM RADIO OPERATION. Sensitive headset picks up strong local radio stations; microphone for at-home broadcasts. Kit contains parts for transistor radio-broadcasting set; includes plastic cabinet, 17½x8½x3½ in., 2¼-in. Alnico speaker, 1500 ohm headphones, diode detector, selective station tuner, wire, other parts. Order three "C" cells below.
48 HT 20051—With instructions. Ship. wt. 4 lbs........Set $8.50

Treasure Probe
Finds Buried Metal
$9.99

TRANSISTORIZED PROBE finds buried treasure, coins and metallic objects up to 2 inches below the surface. Use to explore beaches, deserts, ghost towns; hunt for Indian relics and other buried objects. Sensitive to gold, silver, copper, bronze, iron—detects any metal. Gold finished probe comes with earphone and ore sample. Probe emits an indicating tone when metal is located. 35 inches long, 5½-in. diameter detector unit. Needs one 9-volt battery, order at right. Shipping weight 2 lbs.
48 HT 20023..........$9.99

Big Ear Listening Post $12.00

Works on same principle as missile tracking antennas

POWERFUL TRANSISTORIZED LISTENING DEVICE picks up voices and sounds too distant to hear without aid. Big 18-inch red parabola concentrates sound waves into the transistor unit and amplifies them through stethoscope type earphones. Sturdy wood tripod with balanced aiming handle, 44 in. high. Order 9-volt battery at right.
48 HT 20042M—Ship. wt. 6 lbs..........$12.00

BATTERIES

EXTRA DUTY ALKALINE BATTERIES give up to 8 times longer life than ordinary batteries. Check size needed before ordering.

ALKALINE "D" CELL.
60 T 13267—Wt. of 2, 8 oz. 2,$1.09

ALKALINE "C" CELL.
60 T 13268—Wt. of 2, 6 oz. 2, 99c

LONG LIFE "C" CELL.
60 T 13258—Wt. of 5, 15 oz...5, 75c

HEAVY DUTY "D" CELL.
60GT13265—Wt. of 5, 1¼ lbs. 5, 95c

"AA" PENLITE BATTERY.
60 T 13260—Wt. of 5, 10 oz...5, 75c

9-V. FLAT TRANSISTOR BATTERY.
60 T 13261—Wt. of 2, 8 oz....2, 70c

LARGE 6-V. BATTERY.
60 T 13257—Wt. 1 lb. 12 oz. Ea. 89c

370 SC

1965

Realistic Fighting Gear for Young Commandos

The Johnny Seven
One-Man Army .. Micro-Helmet

Squad Leader Set $3⁹⁹

LEAD YOUR FORCES INTO ACTION with this complete Squad Leader Set. "Burp" gun has exciting trigger sound action, flashing muzzle; helmet has real netting. .45 pistol shoots plastic bullets (included), also fires caps*, fits in belt and holster, 2 cap-firing* grenades. "Burp" gun 18 in. long; .45 pistol 7 in. long. Sturdy plastic.
48 T 3313 M—Shipping weight 3 lbs...... Set $3.99

Micro-Helmet Set Only $4⁹⁷

Detachable Automatic Pistol

Seven Different Weapons In One!

Only $5⁸⁷ At Wards

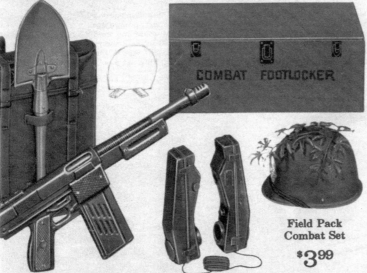

COMBAT FOOTLOCKER

Field Pack Combat Set
$3⁹⁹

ᴸᴸ THE NECESSARY EQUIPMENT FOR THE YOUNG COMMANDO. Dig-in with 19-in. long ᴴᵒvel of durable plastic. Communicate with your buddy on walkie-talkie with two ʳceiver-transmitters and about 30 feet of cord. Set includes aiming tommy gun, ᶜᵒrrugated-board footlocker, dog tags and helmet with camouflage leaves. Heavy duty ᵉld pack of olive-drab duck with elastic shoulder straps fits all sizes.
ᴮ T 3304—Shipping weight 1 lb. 8 oz............................Set $3.99

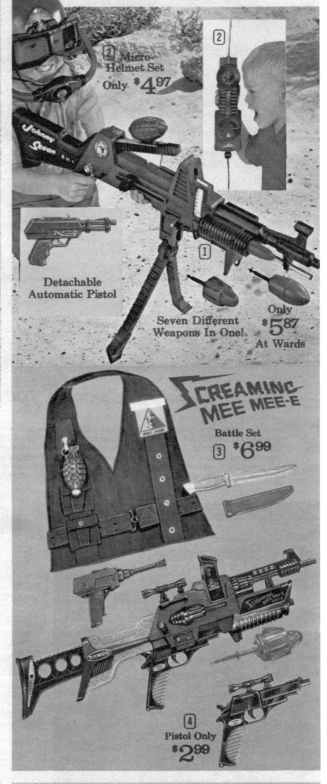

SCREAMING MEE MEE-E
Battle Set
$6⁹⁹

Pistol Only $2⁹⁹

M1 Garand Rifle

REPLICA OF THE WORLD FAMOUS M1 RIFLE fires caps*, has a soft plastic bayonet. Hi-impact plastic, die-cast metal firing mechanism. Over 31 in. long.
48 T 3315 M—Ship. wt. 1 lb. 4 oz......$1.99

$1⁹⁹

RAT-AT-TAT

Tommy Gun $1⁹⁹

1965

IF IT'S MILITARY, WARDS HAS IT!

Johnny Seven

[1] GRENADE LAUNCHER has 3-position range-elevation. Long-range ANTI-TANK ROCKET fires shell by button in forward grip. ARMOR-PIERCING SHELL fired by button at right front of gun. ANTI-BUNKER MISSILE fired at left front of gun. Remove stock and retract bipod legs . . JOHNNY SEVEN becomes an AUTOMATIC REPEATING RIFLE with 12 shells. Use as TOMMY GUN too—makes realistic "rat-tat-tat" sound. Cap-firing* AUTOMATIC PISTOL detaches from main body. Sturdy plastic; gun abt. 36 in. long. Ship. wt. 4 lbs. 9 oz.
48 T 3397 MO—*No batteries needed* . . **$5.87**

[2] JOHNNY SEVEN MICRO-HELMET. Microphone in helmet yoke transmits voice to walkie-talkie through 30 feet of wire (included). *Needs no batteries.* Tinted goggles raise and lower, protect eyes against glare. Adjustable to fit all head sizes.
48 T 3341 MO—Wt. 2 lbs. 7 oz. . . . . . Set **$4.97**

$3.69

Johnny Seven Combat Phones

JOHNNY SEVEN WALKIE TALKIE COMBAT PHONES enable you to contact reinforcements, the tank corps, infantry or headquarters; 30 feet of wire. You can maintain contact with your troops within a one mile range with additional wire. Each phone 14 in. long. Sturdy plastic. *No batteries needed.*
48 T 2288—Ship. wt. 1 lb. 9 oz. **$3.69**

Screaming Mee Mee Battle Set

[3] SHOOT THE GRENADE from the Screaming Mee Mee Rifle . . it actually makes a shrill noise as it screams its way to the target. Feed 5 big rapid-fire bullets into the magazine, slide the bolt and you're ready to fire. Release gunlock, secret pistol drops down for close-range fire—shoots the same screaming grenade. Set incl. rifle, secret pistol, battle jacket of Sanforized® olive drab twill which adjusts to fit all sizes. Knife and sheath fit on belt; "pineapple" grenade is cap-firing*. All weapons of sturdy plastic; rifle abt. 28 in. long.
48 T 3370 M—Ship. wt. 5 lbs. . . . . . . Set **$6.99**

SCREAMING MEE MEE RIFLE ONLY.
48 T 3371 M—Ship. wt. 3 lbs. 8 oz. **$3.99**

[4] SCREAMING MEE MEE PISTOL fires caps* (not incl.) and grenade; abt. 20 in. long.
48 T 3372—Ship. wt. 1 lb. 10 oz. **$2.99**

Tommy Gun

TOMMY GUN WITH SHOULDER SLING. Pull-back bolt-lever sets gun at ready-to-fire. Trigger activates rate of fire. Ejects shells—barrel recoils. Sturdy plastic. About 19 in. long.
48 T 3385 M—Ship. wt. 1 lb. 8 oz. . . **$1.99**

*See "Notice" on Page 272.

1965

Secret Weapons Combat Outfit

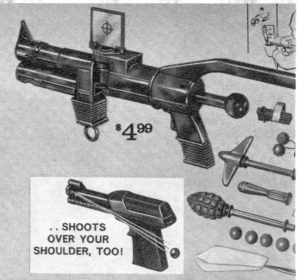

$4.99

COUNTLESS SURPRISE ACTIONS in this new secret weapons combat set: Gun That Shoots Around the Corner, bazooka shell, glider bomb, rifle grenade, parachute, bola shot, 10 soft rubber balls and spotter beam light for night combat (uses 1 "AA" battery, Pg. 354). Gun (abt. 24 in. long) shoots at right angle in either direction. Mirror-sight pivots automatically to sight your target; bolt action moves next shot to firing position. Also includes Pistol That Shoots Over Your Shoulder and 30 poplets. Sturdy plastic. Wt. 3 lbs. 10 oz.
48 T 3436 M—Combat Set. . **$4.99**

GUN WITH 10 BALLS ONLY.
48T3376M—Wt. 1 lb. 10 oz. . **$2.99**

.. SHOOTS OVER YOUR SHOULDER, TOO!

Multi Pistol 09 Just $3.99

MULTI PISTOL 09 has secret derringer cap*-pistol concealed in handle; fires long and short range bullets, "armor-piercing" shell, message capsule, exploding grenade and torpedo bomb with cap-detonator. Optical sight really works; barrel extension gives long-range accuracy. Beautifully designed plastic case. Gun abt. 11 in. long, sturdy plastic.
48 T 3433—Ship. wt. 2 lbs. . . . **$3.99**

Big Cat $6.99

THE ONLY MOVABLE WEAPON WITH A BARREL [THAT] REALLY RETRACTS! Roll it along with the barre[l posi]tioned to pounce. Enemy sighted! Crank barrel [to] its full sweeping 35 inches (as shown) . . Big Ca[t] automatically. Adjust elevation, load shell[s.] FIRE! Open breech, casing automatically [eject.] Sturdy plastic with 3 shells, 2 casings.
48 T 3435 M—Ship. wt. 9 lbs. . . . .

Gung Ho Outfit

ACTION-PACKED REPLICA OF .50 CALIBER MACHINE GUN with recoiling barrel, flashing muzzle and firing noise. "Ammunition belt" moves as gun is fired. Sturdy plastic, abt. 28 in. long. Over 30 pcs.: knap-sack with canteen, mess kit, compass, .45 automatic pistol, walkie talkie, dagger with sheath, grenades, battle map, map case, etc. Order 3 "D" batteries, Page 354.
48 T 3384 M—Ship. wt. 7 lbs. **$8.44**

Gung Ho Commando Outfit

Only $8.44

Talk-N-Walkie Talkie

$2.79

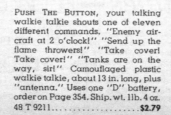

PUSH THE BUTTON, your talking walkie talkie shouts one of eleven different commands. "Enemy aircraft at 2 o'clock!" "Send up the flame throwers!" "Take cover! Take cover!" "Tanks are on the way, sir!" Camouflaged plastic walkie talkie, about 13 in. long, plus "antenna." Uses one "D" battery, order on Page 354. Ship. wt. 1lb. 4 oz.
48 T 9211 . . . . **$2.79**

C3 WARDS

Introducing
SECRET SUE ©

© 1965, 1966
Cherry & Shackleford
Creations, Inc.

Who's Secret Sue?
She's your little girl . . .
leading a breathtaking
double life with Secret Sue
toys and clothes . . .
exclusive at Wards!

Secret Sue Doll $3.00

DRESSED IN HER OWN TRENCH COAT AND BOOTS, this cute red-head is ready to go along with your Secret Sue—whether she's being a special agent or a sweet little girl. 12 in. tall, vinyl jointed body, rooted hair, painted eyes.
48 HT 10202—Wt. 13 oz. . . Secret Sue Doll $3.00

17-Pc. WARDROBE has dresses, slacks that match little girl's fashions A, C and D on opposite page. Includes 5 outfits, plus tiny phone, radio, compass, binoculars, etc.
48 HT 11011—Ship. wt. 10 oz. . . . . . Outfit $3.50

Tiny Sue with Trunk $3.50

JUST LIKE BIG SECRET SUE, with her own tiny trench-coat and dark glasses. She's only 4 in. high, with molded vinyl body, rooted hair. Has her own little blue trunk so you can carry her anywhere. 4 dresses on little pink hangers to keep them neat. Ship. wt. 8 oz.
48 HT 10441—Doll, Trunk and Clothes $3.50

Secret Sue Costume $5.00

ALL GOOD LITTLE "SECRET AGENTS" need proper attire and equipment . . . and our play costume has everything she needs to start sleuthing! Beige cotton drill spy-type trench coat (like worn by Secret Sue doll at right) has black belt; white "spats" fit over shoes for boot effect. Bright orange-red wig, special disguise glasses, black simulated leather over-the-shoulder bag all included with costume. (Hat-box sold separately below.) *State Size:* Small, Medium, Large (size table on Page 255).
Z48 HT 35000—Ship. wt. 1 lb. 4 oz. . . . . Secret Sue Costume $5.00

RED AND WHITE STRIPED VINYL COVERED HAT BOX has all-around zipper that opens to divulge a hidden telephone, a real camera, flashlight, decoder wheel, notebook, etc. . . . all the equipment needed for checking clues, gathering evidence, reporting to headquarters.
48 HT 11727—10½-in. diam., 7 in. deep. Ship. wt. 1 lb. 11 oz. . . . . Hat Box $5.00

Secret Sue's own pendant watch

$10.95

DESIGNED ESPECIALLY FOR GIRL SLEUTHS, with Secret Sue's name and 2 red hearts on face. Swiss movement, white pearlized dial, black numerals, hands. Gold-color metal case, chain.
45 HT 209—Ship. wt. 8 oz. . . . . Watch only $10.95

16 WARDS ALL

1966

and SECRET SUE FASHIONS

Heather Coordinates
Size 7 Petite

A $2.99

B $5.97

C $3.99

D $3.99

E $1.99

F $9.99

G $2.99

Little Girl Fashions to match the clothes worn by the Secret Sue Doll

A To Catch a Spy Secret Sue wears a pullover jumper of wide wale cotton corduroy. White top-stitching and brass buttons add a dash of fashion. Inverted front action pleat. Machine wash medium.
Colors: 520 red or 514 navy.
Sizes: 4, 5, 6, 6x. State color no., size.
B31 T 4805—Ship. wt. 8 oz **$2.99**

B Vinyl Boot has secret side pocket. Tricot lining. Back zipper. White. Width C: Sizes: 10-4. Half sizes, too.
Z24T4903—Wt. 1 lb. 4 oz. State size. **$5.97**

C Spies Beware! Secret Sue is on the scene in her cotton poplin A-line dress. Delicate embroidery trims white collar and cuffs. Inverted front pleat. Back zipper. Machine wash, medium. *State color number and size.*
Colors: 514 navy or 520 red.
Sizes: 4, 5, 6, 6x.
B31 T 6505—Ship. wt. 8 oz **$3.99**

Accessories: See Big Fall Book. Shoes: Pg. 425, Socks: Pg. 450, Tights: Pg. 439. To Measure for Secret Sue Fashions, See Big Fall Book, Page 387.

D Secret Sue Goes Sleuthing in a wide wale cotton corduroy slack set. Double breasted weskit tops cuffed pants. Pants have band front waist, elastic back. Machine wash med. Ship. wt. 9 oz.
Colors: 514 navy or 520 red.
Sizes: 4, 5, 6, 6x.
B31T4260-State color no.,size.**$3.99**

E Ribbed Cotton Knit Top for all her sportswear. Machine wash med. Sizes: 4, 5, 6, 6x. Ship. wt. 6 oz.
Z31 T 4262-White. State size.**$1.99**

F The Trench Coat in water repellent cotton poplin, shoulder epaulets. Body is warmly acrylic pile lined (cotton back). Quilted sleeves, two welt pockets. Buckle belt. Hand wash. Ship. wt. 1 lb. 4 oz.
Sizes: 4, 5, 6, 6x.
Z31 T 8488—Navy only. State size. **$9.99**

G Cotton Poplin Hat. Ear laps, chin-tie. Sizes: M (19½–20¼), L (20½–21½). Color: navy (as shown). Ship. wt. 5 oz.
Z31 T 9280—State M or L **$2.99**

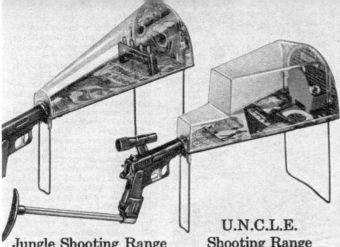

Jungle Shooting Range
$3⁰⁰

Shoots as fast as you can pull the trigger! To score, shoot into the open jaws of the molded lion or hippo heads . . . or knock over the panels in front of them. Exciting, competitive, challenging. Self-loading, plastic automatic fires metal pellets. Clear plastic case encloses game. Metal legs. Abt. 19x7½x12¼ in. high. Wt. 2 lbs. 6 oz.
48 HT 14710 . . . . $3.00

U.N.C.L.E. Shooting Range
$3⁶⁶

Be an international Special Agent. Help Napoleon Solo and Illya eliminate Thrush agents. Napoleon's distinctive gun has 15-in. stock extension and peep sight, fires metal pellets. Attached to moving target. Wind-up motor, clear plastic housing. Abt. 13¼ x7¼x4¾ in. wide. Metal legs. Ship. wt. 2 lbs. 5 oz.
48 HT 14709 . . . . $3.66

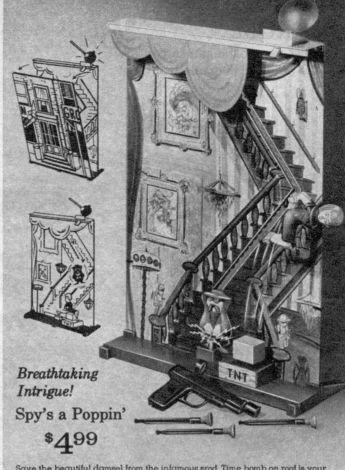

Breathtaking Intrigue!
Spy's a Poppin'
$4⁹⁹

Save the beautiful damsel from the infamous spy! Time bomb on roof is your first target—shoot it, front of the house falls. The interior looks peaceful, but the infra red sight on your plastic pistol reveals spies hiding behind the pictures. Shoot them—master spy "runs" down from attic. Shoot him before he can reach plunger on T.N.T. chest or girl will be blown into the air!
48HT14707M—Abt. 18x24 in. high. 3 rubber-tipped darts. Wt. 4 lbs. 5 oz. $4.99

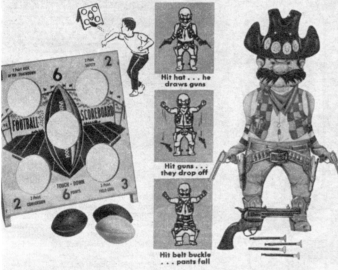

Hit hat . . . he draws guns

Hit guns . . . they drop off

Hit belt buckle . . . pants fall

Football Toss
$3⁵⁰

Try for a touchdown! Toss your football through any of 5 holes—each gives a different score. Sturdy wood scoreboard about 18x18 in. with easel stand. 3 colored plastic footballs. For ages 5 and up. Ship. wt. 4 lbs.
48 HT 14700 M $3.50

Hands Up Harry
$3⁹⁹

Harry responds to direct hits, and the final shot brings down his pants to reveal his bright, candy-striped shorts. Plastic western dart gun, 4 suction-cup darts. 28-in. tall masonite target. Ship. wt. 4 lbs. 6 oz.
48 HT 14708 M $3.99

Score added up automatically as you play

SKEE BALL
The popular Carnival skill game
$3⁸⁸

Rabbit Hunt
$2⁶⁶

Wind up the rabbit and set him to go in circles or straight. Try to hit him on the run with one of the rubber-tipped darts. Motor stops when you knock him down. Realistic-looking mechanical rabbit is sturdy plastic. 23½ in. double-barreled plastic shot gun shoots one dart, or two at a time.
48 HT 14706 M—3 harmless suction-cup darts incl. Ship. wt. 2 lbs. 8 oz. $2.66

Pull the handle and try to shoot the ball through the air into the highest scoring hole. The favorite Carnival game scaled down to toy-chest size. Looks like the real thing, plays like the real thing. For ages 6 and up. Sturdy metal. Abt. 28¾x11x16½ in. high.
48 HT 14711 M—Ship. wt. 6 lbs. $3.88

1966

Transmits up to one mile!
8-Transistor Walkie-Talkies

No ear plugs or wires . . .
Clear, long distance reception

$13³³
Each
in pairs

Now You Can Have a Wireless communication system that's more than just a toy. These powerful units transmit up to one mile under ideal conditions. Anyone can operate them without any examination or license. Just pull out the telescoping antenna to its full 49-inch length. Press button and speak clearly and distinctly into the speaker-microphone; release button to listen. With full volume control and on-off switch. Optional squelch circuit reduces background noise from your conversations when talking over 100 feet apart. Operates on frequency controlled to citizens broadcast band, channel 14. Will receive messages from other space phones within range, transmitting on channel 14, as well as police calls and ham radio broadcasts nearby. Transistorized transmitter and receiver. Lightweight die-cast aluminum case. Black with chrome finished trim. Order one 9-volt battery, on opposite page, for each unit. Ship. wt. 1 lb. each.
48 HT 20021–Ea $14.99; 2, $26.66

A Charming Gift? See Page 66

Signature Jr. 4-Transistor Wireless Walkie-Talkie
$7⁴⁴
Each
in pairs

Clear 2-Way Conversations up to ½ mile away. Keeps the youngsters busy for hours. Great for grownups too—use for family outings, camping, fishing and hunting trips—use in boats, car or on bicycles. Lightweight and small, they fit comfortably in the hand; 6¾x1¾x2½ in. Press button and speak into bottom grill; release button and listen at top grill. With 46-in. telescoping antenna and on-off switch.

Anyone can operate them, no examination or license required, no age limit. Operates on frequency controlled to citizens broadcast band, channel 14. Picks up messages sent from nearby transmitters, such as police calls and ham operators. Shock resistant snap-open plastic case. Order one 9-volt battery (opp. pg.) for each unit. Order 2 or more for multi-way conversations. Ship. wt. ea. 13 oz.
48HT20020—Each $8.99; 2 for $14.88

6-Transistor Radio
$4⁴⁹

Personal Size Radio, goes where you go. Compact, 1¼x4¼x2¹¹⁄₁₆ in., permits carrying in shirt pocket or purse. Comes with handy wrist strap to help prevent misplacing or dropping radio.

Heavy-duty speaker carries sound loud and clear. Highly sensitive, with built-in aerial. Convenient direct drive tuning. Charcoal trim on blue, high-impact case. Earphone permits private listening that won't disturb others. Uses one 9-volt battery, order on opposite page.
48 HT 20005—Ship. wt. 10 oz. $4.49

1966

Bullet Fires Through Closed Case

Slide-Out, Concealed Flexible Dagger

Secret Lock Explodes When Case is Opened by Enemy

"James Bond 007©" Attaché Case

A Fully Equipped Special Assignment Attaché Case

ONLY $6⁹⁹

THIS RUGGED LEATHER-GRAINED MOLDED PLASTIC CASE looks innocent enough, but is packed with secret features .. has concealed trigger that fires bullet .. "explodes" if opened by an enemy agent .. conceals a flexible dagger. Included inside case are a 30-in. 4-piece rifle that assembles in seconds .. fires automatically .. serves as a "Shoulder-stock Automatic Weapon," an Automatic Pistol, a single-shot Luger-type Pistol and a "Silencer." The Code-O-Matic contains 4 different codes and message paper. There's a booby trap code book that "explodes" when opened by an enemy, a passport, international currency, and a secret compartment to conceal valuable papers. The attaché case fires plastic bullet. The booby trap mechanisms fire paper caps.*

48 T 3458—Ship. wt. 5 lbs. . . . . SET $6.99
48 T 3459—RIFLE ONLY. Ship. wt. 1 lb. 8 oz. . . 2.99

Jet Coder

Camera Opens into a Pistol

Zero-M Sonic-Blaster $7⁹⁹

Zero-M Night-Fighter $2⁹⁹

"Camera" Pistol .. Jet Coder $2⁸⁸

ZERO-M SONIC-BLASTER. "Agent Zero-M's" most powerful new weapon. Pump the handle until the Sonic-Blaster signals it is ready with a "hiss." Then aim and fire. A harmless blast of air will actually put out a match up to 40 feet away, scatter newspaper. Airport target actually "blows up" when hit by blast of air. Blaster about 3 feet long, hi-impact plastic and metal, with working-sight for precision aiming. Complete cardboard airport is ready to assemble; rubber bands included.
48 T 3438 M—Ship. wt. 4 lbs. 14 oz. . . . . SET $7.99

ZERO-M NIGHT-FIGHTER for the night-fighting secret agent. New cap-firing* submachine gun for "Agent Zero-M." Fires 50 perforated roll caps* in bursts or single shots. Smooth-working repeater bolt action. The adjustable Infra-Scope is a see-through telescopic sight. Flash guard barrel to hide firing flashes. Smoking barrel; simulated silencer. About 25 inches long. Durable hi-impact plastic has an authentic-looking camouflage finish.
48 T 3444 M—Ship. wt. 1 lb. 8 oz. $2.99

ZERO-M "CAMERA" PISTOL looks like an ordinary camera—becomes a cap-firing* pistol when danger approaches. Snap shutter .. barrel and pistol grip pop out. Push them back to re-disguise secret pistol as a camera. High-impact black and silver plastic. ZERO-M JET CODER. Plastic ball-point pen writes secret messages, shoots powerful stream of water. Write secret message using white cartridge, then write ordinary message over it using red cartridge. Put on special glasses—only secret message shows.
48 T 3445—Ship. wt. 1 lb. . . . . SET $2.88

Man from U.N.C.L.E.

$3⁹⁹

"MAN FROM U.N.C.L.E." GUN WITH HOLSTER. This UNCLE cap-firing* basic .45 automatic toy pistol looks ordinary until you convert it into a special UNCLE rifle. Fast clip-loading .. clip slides into pistol grip. Barrel extension has a built-in silencer. Bi-pod legs attach to extended barrel for extra balance. Slip on the Superscope telescopic sight for accurate aiming and fire. Smoke rolls from barrel when roll caps* are fired. Authentically detailed in rugged plastic and metal. UNCLE badge, I.D. card included.
48 T 3467—Ship. wt. 1 lb. 12 oz. . . . . . . SET $3.99

*See Notice Page 272.

1966

ZING

KA-PINNG

① Ricochet rifle
4⁷⁶

② Crrackfire rifle
3⁹⁹

Poppin rifle ③
2⁹⁹

④ Smoke rifle
3⁴⁹

Saddle rifles with realistic effects

① **Daisy ricochet smoke rifle.** Rifle sings out with ricochet sound and bangs as smoke curls out of the barrel. No caps or batteries required. Just cock the lever and pull trigger. Durable steel construction with wood-grained plastic stock. About 30 in. long.
48 HT 19300 M—Ship. wt. 3 lbs............4.76

② **Crrackfire rifle.** A really authentic rifle shot and ricochet sound. Needs no batteries or caps. Just pull the trigger and sound emits from grill on left side of stock. Sounds taken from western movie sound track. Made of plastic, about 30 in. long, with wood-grained stock. Designed to look like the Winchester '94.
48 HT 19024 M—Ship. wt. 2 lbs. 6 oz.........3.99

③ **Daisy "poppin" rifle.** 30-in. long lever action hunting rifle with gold-colored steel play scope. Shoots plastic "poppin" bullets (tapered corks) with loud pop sound. (5 included.) Real hardwood stock extends under the barrel. Steel barrel and receiver. Ventilated rib, magazine and adjustable sling.
48 HT 19302 M—Ship. wt. 2 lbs. 6 oz...........2.99

④ **Daisy smoke rifle.** Makes a loud bang, smokes and even recoils when you fire it, just like a real rifle. Uses no caps or batteries. Cock with simple lever action mechanism. Wood-grained plastic stock with metal barrel and frame. About 30 inches long.
48 HT 19301 M—Ship. wt. 2 lbs. 8 oz...........3.49

Phone your order. See page 346

⑤

⑦

⑥

For the bunkhouse

⑤ **Trusty palomino** helps him keep his room neat. Saddlebags are packed with comb, toothbrush, nail file and nail clippers. Unbreakable plastic. Abt. 7 in. high.
53 HT 12252—Ship. wt. 12 oz...........2.6

⑥ **Cowboy's clothes horse.** Walnut finished wood clothes tree is child-sized, about 4 feet tall. A handy room addition which gives a child interest in neatness.
53 HT 18795 M—Ship. wt. 3 lbs.........3.4

⑦ **Wagon wheel wall clothes rack.** Woodton plastic wagon wheel has 6 horseshoe for hooks with leather thongs. Imitation steerhorn at top of rack for caps and ties.
53 HT 18796—Ship. wt. 2 lbs. 8 oz......3.4

Complete
spy set **4⁹⁹**

Hardware for
little big-shots **2⁹⁹**

Movie-Shot and Snap-Shot look like ordinary cameras until a snap of the shutter makes them a cap firing* machine gun and pistol. Movie-Shot with 2-pc. telescoping barrel, fires in bursts or single shots, has handy plastic carrying case. Both black and silver high-impact plastic. Includes Zero-M Jet Coder that writes secret messages; and special decoding glasses.
48 HT 19715—Ship. wt. 2 lbs. 14 oz...........set 4.99

Pint-sized pistols and rifle for little range riders. Genuine leather holsters decorated with concha and jewel. Adjustable belt fits smallest cowboy. Die-cast pistols. Rifle fires roll caps* and ejects harmless plastic bullets.
48 HT 19416 M—Ship. wt. 1 lb. 12 oz...set 2.99

*See "Notice" on page 215

Magic ray gun for family fun $15

Durable plastic rifle fires harmless beam of light. If you hit the bull's eye on the target a bell rings and the pointer spins around coming to rest on a number for score. Rifle uses 3 "D" cell batteries; target uses 4 "D" cell batteries, not incl. Order page 288. Rifle about 30 in. long.
48 HT 19710 A**—Ship. wt. 5 lbs. 8 oz......................set 15.00

**Mailable to some locations.
See AID page 345 for explanation.

1967

Dress up— join the parade!

Batman
5⁸⁷

Save 50%

Visiting Nurse 3⁷⁹

Crisp white button-down dress is washable. Navy blue cotton cape with insignia. Perky cap. Plastic shoulder bag. Ship. wt. 1 lb. 2 oz. *State size: S, M, or L.*
Z 48 HT 35016.........3.79

Man from U.N.C.L.E. 3⁹⁹

Vinyl trench coat with over a dozen secret pockets for weapons and disguises. With attaché case and more than 20 intriguing spy items. Wt. 3 lbs. 10 oz. *State size: S, M or L.*
Z 48 HT 35014—Was 7.99..3.99

Superman 5⁸⁷

A bird? a plane?—it's Superman! Red cape, blue shirt with shield, long pants with elastic top, belt. Washable cotton. Ship. wt. 1 lb. 2 oz. *State size: S, M or L.*
Z 48 HT 35004.........5.87

Be sure to measure—see Size Chart on opposite page. Cowboy outfits are on page 199.

Jaunty majorette

4⁸⁹

Toot the whistle, twirl the baton and lead off! Smart outfit is washable cotton—jacket has gold-color trim, metal buttons. Skirt has elastic back. Fur-like hat, plastic boots. Wt. 1 lb. 8 oz. *State: S, M or L.*
Z 48 HT 35002...........4.89

Batman official outfit, utility belt

Pow! Zonk! Batman's fighting crime! Washable cotton outfit: swirling cape, shirt, pants, belt, hood and mask.
Z 48 HT 35015—*State size: S, M or L.* Ship. wt. 1 lb. 2 oz...5.87

Belt holds plastic "wonder weapons": rope, grappling hook; grenade; pretend 2-way radio buckle, secret compartment; Bat gun, message sender; Batarang; Batcuffs, etc.
48 HT 35500—Batman utility belt. Ship. wt. 3 lbs, 6 oz....4.66

Belt

4⁶⁶

NEW!
Exclusive at Wards
FORT HERO

Complete outfit
7⁹⁹
Save 1.58
Separately 9.57

Relive the Old West with frontier outpost, covered wagon, 6-in. American hero cavalrymen.

Hours of imaginative fun and action at Ft. Hero! Send out a scout, unload the supply wagon, defend the fort from marauders. Flexible plastic SOLDIERS with accesories can be bent and twisted into live action positions. Their Western pony has saddle, bridle and stirrups. Big FORT is lithographed cardboard with general store, stockade, ammunition and storage lockers. Abt. 24 in. square. COVERED WAGON, with two horses, is plastic, cloth cover, abt. 20 in. long overall. About 10 realistic accessories.

48 HT 24449—**Two 6-in. cavalrymen** with accessories, one fully equipped horse. Wt. 1 lb. 2.59

48 HT 24606—**Covered wagon** with two horses, realistic supplies. Ship. wt. 2 lbs........4.99

48 HT 24675 M—**Fort.** Ship. wt. 1 lb. 8 oz....1.99

Complete outfit. Separately 9.57, Save 1.58.
48 HT 24676 MM—Ship. wt. 4 lbs. 9 oz....7.99

200 WARDS sc

1967

Spy Fan Clubs and Websites

SPY TOYS AND COLLECTIBLES

www.spyguise.com - A virtual spy department store of new and old movie and television spy collectibles including books, posters and toys.

JAMES BOND 007

www.jamesbond.com - The Official James Bond Website from MGM/UA. A state of the art site with all the news about the latest 007 project as well as a line of Bond movie merchandise.

www.ianfleming.org - The Ian Fleming Foundation, P.O. Box 1850, Burbank, California 91507. Publishers of *GOLDENEYE MAGAZINE*. A great deal of 007 memorabilia and terrific merchandise for sale too.

www.thejamesbondfanclub.com - The James Bond International Fan Club, P.O. Box 007, Addlestone, Surrey KT15 1DY England. A superb British-based Bond fan club. Publishers of *007 MAGAZINE* and offers a wide range of merchandise.

THE MAN FROM U.N.C.L.E.

www.uncle.org - The Fans From U.N.C.L.E. Everything you could possibly want to know about U.N.C.L.E., its stars and news updates.

THE AVENGERS

www.OriginalAvengers.com - A wonderful site dedicated to the British spy duo. The latest news about Steed and Peel and the best source for remastered TV episodes on home video.

WILD, WILD WEST

www.uvm.edu/~glambert/twww1.html - Contains TV schedules, cast biographies, news updates and mailing list for the classic television series.

SECRET AGENT

www.dspace.dial.pipex.com/town/place/gu93/triv.htm - A loyal fan's website, with tons of background information and full credits.

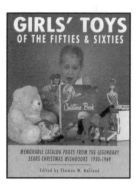

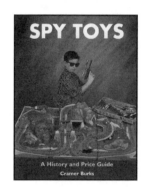